OCS EIS/EA
MMS 2001-097

Environmental Assessment

Proposed OCS Lease Sale 182, Central Gulf of Mexico

I0428128

Author

Minerals Management Service
Gulf of Mexico OCS Region

U.S. Department of the Interior
Minerals Management Service
Gulf of Mexico OCS Region

**New Orleans
October 2001**

Finding of No New Significant Impacts

The Minerals Management Service (MMS) has prepared an environmental assessment (EA) for proposed Lease Sale 182 in the Central Planning Area of the Gulf of Mexico Outer Continental Shelf (OCS). The EA was prepared to determine whether or not the information and analyses in the Final EIS for Proposed Lease Sales 169,172,175, 178, and 182 (multisale EIS) have changed sufficiently to warrant further analysis for proposed Sale 182 in the Central Gulf of Mexico. Because the multisale EIS examined the environmental impacts of a sale similar in size, nature, and potential level of development as Sale 182, this EA tiers off the initial multisale EIS and incorporates much of the material by reference. It also reexamines the potential environmental effects of the proposed action and alternatives based on any new information regarding potential impacts or issues that were not available at the time the Final EIS was prepared.

The information and analysis presented in the multisale EIS were reviewed. Three topics were determined to have new information requiring a reevaluation of the environmental impact analysis: socioeconomics, essential fish habitat, and piping plover critical habitat. The new information is presented in the EA. Also presented is an analysis based on the new information, prepared to determine if the kinds, levels, or locations of impacts foreseen in the multisale EIS would significantly change.

Based on the analyses in the EA, no new significant impacts were identified for proposed Lease Sale 182 that were not already assessed in the multisale EIS, nor was it necessary to change the conclusions of the kinds, levels, or locations of impacts described in the multisale EIS. Therefore, the MMS has determined that a supplemental EIS to the multisale EIS is not required and is issuing this Finding of No New Significant Impacts.

Supporting Documents:

> The EA for Proposed OCS Lease Sale 182, Central Gulf of Mexico (attached).
>
> Final Environmental Impact Statement, Gulf of Mexico, Central Gulf of Mexico OCS Oil and Gas Lease Sales 169, 172, 175, 178, and 182, November, 1997 (available upon request).

Thomas R Kitsos
Director

10/36/01
Date

TABLE OF CONTENTS

I. OBJECTIVES OF THE ENVIRONMENTAL ASSESSMENT

This environmental assessment (EA) was prepared to determine whether or not the information and analyses in the multisale environmental impact statement (EIS) have changed sufficiently to warrant further analysis for proposed Sale 182 in the Central Gulf of Mexico. The EA tiers off the initial multisale EIS and incorporates all of the relevant material by reference.

It also reexamines the potential environmental effects of the proposed action and alternatives based on any new information regarding potential impacts and issues not available at the time MMS prepared the November 1997, Final Environmental Impact Statement EIS for Central Planning Area (CPA) Lease Sales 169, 172, 175, 178, and 182 (USDOI, MMS, 1997).

Federal regulations allow for an agency to analyze several similar proposals in one EIS (40 CFR 1502.4). Since the Gulf of Mexico sale proposal and projected activities are very similar, if not almost identical each year, the MMS prepared a single EIS for all five Central Gulf sales in the 5-Year Program. The multisale approach focuses the NEPA/EIS process on any differences between the proposed sales and on any new information and issues. Although the multisale EIS addressed five proposed sale actions, the Secretary makes only one sale decision each year.

II. PURPOSE AND NEED FOR THE PROPOSAL

Purpose

The purpose of the proposed action is to make available for leasing those areas that may contain economically recoverable oil and gas resources in the CPA of the Gulf of Mexico for energy use in the United States (U.S.).

Need for the Proposed Action

The Central Gulf of Mexico constitutes one of the world's major oil and gas producing areas and has proved to be a steady and reliable source of crude oil and natural gas for more than 50 years. Oil and gas from the Gulf of Mexico can help reduce the nation's need for oil imports and reduce the environmental risks associated with oil tankering.

III. THE PROPOSED ACTION AND ALTERNATIVES

A. ALTERNATIVE A — PROPOSED ACTION

The proposed Lease Sale 182 planning area includes about 47.8 million acres (ac) located 4.8 to 354 kilometers (km) offshore in water depths ranging from 4 to 3,400 meters (m) (Figure 1). Proposed Sale 182 would offer for lease all available unleased blocks in the CPA except for blocks beyond the United States Exclusive Economic Zone (EEZ) in the area referred to as the northern portion of the Eastern Gap. The MMS had deferred leasing of blocks beyond the EEZ in each of the Gulf of Mexico OCS sale since Sale 169. In Sale 178 Part 2 and Sale 180, MMS offered blocks beyond the EEZ in the Western Gap. On June 9, 2000, following extensive negotiations, the Presidents of the U.S. and Mexico signed a treaty establishing the continental

2

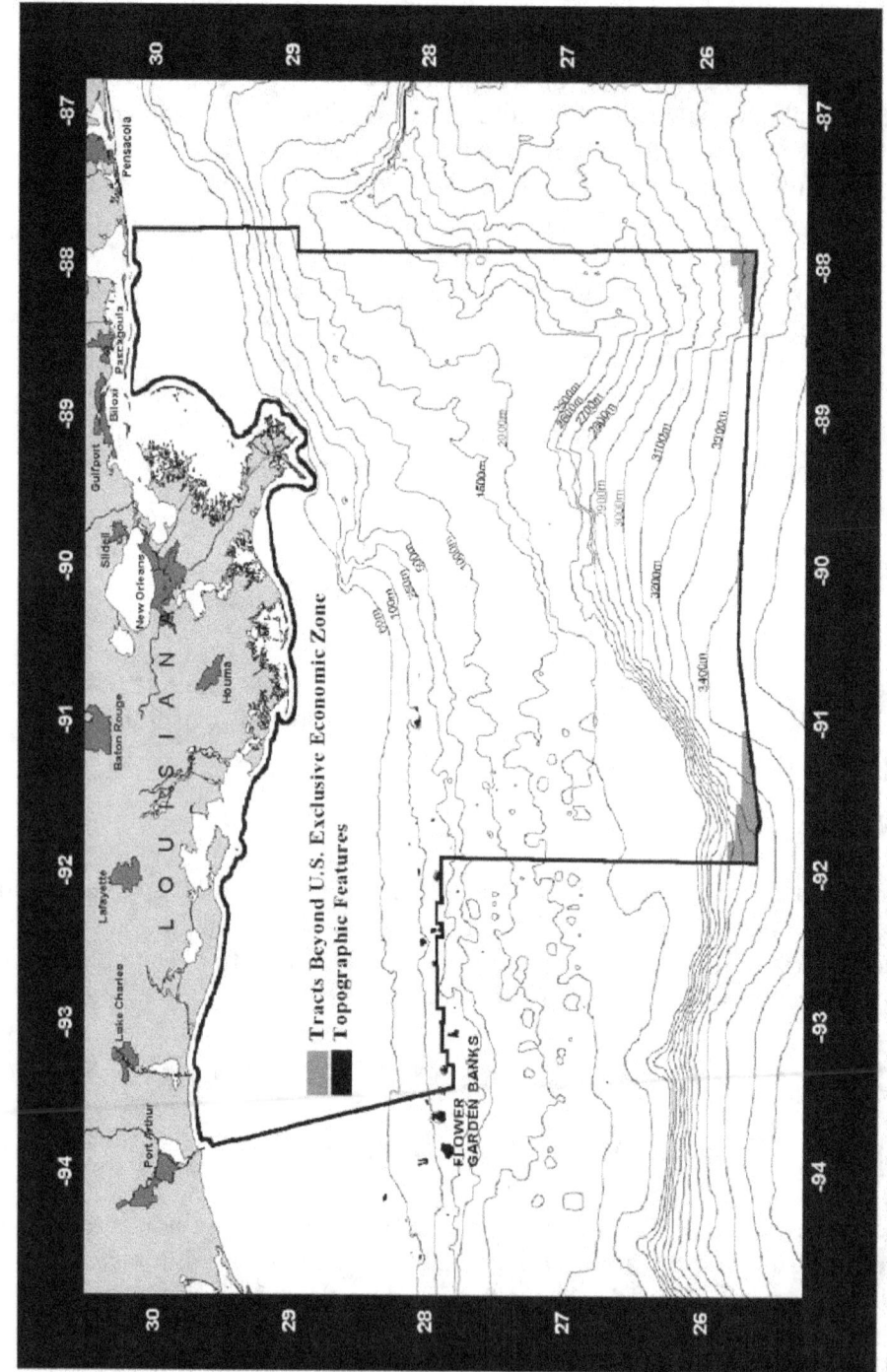

Figure 1. Gulf of Mexico Outer Continental Shelf Central Planning Area and Location of Some Major Cities.

shelf boundary in the Western Gap. Also established is a 1.4-mi buffer zone on each side of the boundary in which the parties agreed to a 10-year moratorium on oil and gas exploitation commencing when the treaty enters into force. The U.S. Senate ratified the treaty on October 18, 2000, and the Mexican Senate gave its approval on November 28, 2000. The agreement is known as the Treaty Between the Government of the United States of America and the Government of the United Mexican States on the Delimitation of the Continental Shelf in the Western Gulf of Mexico Beyond 200 Nautical Miles. The provisions of the treaty entered into force upon exchange of the instruments of ratification of the treaty on January 17, 2001. The MMS proposes to offer the blocks in the area formerly known as the Western Gap but presents an alternative to defer blocks in the Eastern Gap. The following whole and/or partial blocks in the Western Gap area will be offered for lease in addition to all unleased blocks in the CPA. A complete listing of these whole and partial blocks will be included in the Proposed and Final Notices of Sale for the Sale 182 offering.

Additional whole and/or partial blocks that will be offered in this sale are as follows:

Amery Terrace Area Blocks (NG 15-09)

133 through 135
177 through 184
221 through 238
265 through 279
309 through 317

Portions of the following blocks that lie within the 1.4-nmi buffer zone and will NOT be offered in this sale are as follows:

Amery Terrace Area Blocks (NG 15-09)

235 through 238
273 through 279
309 through 317

The proposed action and all subsequent activities resulting from it are subject to the existing regulations and proposed lease stipulations designed to reduce environmental risks. Three stipulations (Live Bottom (Pinnacle Trend), Topographic Features, and Military Areas Stipulations) that have been applied by the Secretary to certain Central Gulf OCS leases for many years are included in the analysis for the proposed actions in the Final EIS for CPA Lease Sales 169, 172, 175, 178, and 182 (USDOI, MMS, 1997). Section II.C.1.c. of the Final EIS discusses the effectiveness of the stipulations. An additional stipulation was added to Lease Sale 169. The MMS, in consultation with the State of Alabama, developed Stipulation No. 4 for Mobile Blocks 826 and 829. The Geological Survey of Alabama conducted a study of methods that could provide for the development of potential hydrocarbons from blocks in the 15-mi area without the installation of new visible structures on the blocks. As a result, these two blocks were offered in Sale 169 with a special stipulation attached. In Lease Sale 172, this stipulation was attached to three additional unleased blocks (Mobile Blocks 957, 958, and 1001). Since then, however, two additional blocks (Mobile Blocks 871 and 962) were relinquished and will have this stipulation attached as well. The stipulation assures that any exploration and development activity on the blocks will be conducted in a manner that minimizes any visual impacts to the Alabama coast. At present, Mississippi Canyon Blocks 871 and 874 are leased and Stipulation No. 4 applies. Mississippi Canyon Blocks 829, 873, 913, 957, 958, 962, 1001, 1002, 1003, 1004, and 1006, and Viosca Knoll Block 35 are unleased. In addition, the MMS's Gulf of Mexico OCS Regional Office agreed to consult with the Alabama State Oil and Gas Board prior to installation of new fixed structures on all blocks in the CPA within 15 mi of the Baldwin County coast.

The MMS estimates that this proposed sale could result in the production of 0.15 to 0.44 billion barrels of oil (BBO) and 1.53 to 4.39 trillion cubic feet (tcf) of gas. The MMS assumes a 35-year life of the leases resulting from the proposed action. Exploratory activity takes place over a 25-year period, beginning in the year of the sale. Development activity takes place over a 29-year period, beginning with the installation of the first production platform and ending with the drilling of the last development wells. Production of oil and gas begins by the second year after a proposed action and continues through the 34th year. Final abandonment and removal activities could begin about 2011 and would continue, as structures cease producing economically, resulting in removal of all projected platforms by the last year of the life of the leases.

B. ALTERNATIVES TO THE PROPOSED ACTION

Alternative B — The Proposed Action Excluding the Blocks Near Biologically Sensitive Topographic Features: Alternative B differs from Alternative A (the proposed action) by not offering the 70 unleased blocks of the 167 total blocks that the proposed Topographic Features Stipulation affects. All the assumptions, including the potential mitigating measures and resource estimates, remain the same as in the proposed action (Alternative A).

Alternative C — The Proposed Action Excluding the Unleased Blocks Within 15 Miles of the Baldwin County, Alabama, Coast: Alternative C differs from Alternative A (the proposed action) by not offering any unleased blocks within 15 mi of the Baldwin County, Alabama, coast (as of September 2001, 12 blocks were unleased). All the assumptions, including the potential mitigating measures and resource estimates, remain the same as in the proposed action (Alternative A).

Alternative D — The Proposed Action Excluding the Blocks in the Eastern Gap: Alternative D differs from Alternative A (the proposed action) by not offering any unleased blocks in an area beyond the U.S. EEZ, known as the northern portion of the Eastern Gap (28 blocks in Lund South, NG 16-7). All the assumptions, including the mitigating measures and resource estimates, remain the same as in the proposed action (Alternative A).

Alternative E — No Action: Alternative E would cancel the lease sale tentatively scheduled for March 2002 on the approved *Outer Continental Shelf Oil and Gas Leasing Program: 1997-2002*. Cancellation of the proposed Central Gulf sale would postpone or forego the opportunity for development of the estimated 0.15 to 0.44 BBO and 1.53 to 4.39 tcf of gas.

IV. IMPACT ANALYSIS

A. UPDATE OF PROJECTIONS OF POTENTIAL ACTIVITY FROM THE PROPOSED ACTION

The Final EIS for CPA Lease Sales 169, 172, 175, 178, and 182 (the multisale EIS) discussed projections for activities associated with a typical proposed action. Review of these projections carried out since the publication of the Final EIS indicates that the information is still valid; MMS therefore incorporates it by reference.

In general, a proposed action represents 1.5 to 3.0 percent of the Gulfwide OCS Program based on barrels of oil equivalent (BOE) resource estimates. Based on averages for time required for exploration, development, production life, and abandonment for leases in the Gulf of Mexico, MMS assumes a 35-year life for the leases resulting from the proposed sale.

The MMS bases projections used to develop the proposed action and OCS Program scenarios on resource and reserves estimates as presented in the *Summary of the 1995 Assessment of Conventionally Recoverable Hydrocarbon Resources of the Gulf of Mexico and Atlantic Outer Continental Shelf* (Lore et al., 1996), current industry information, and observed trends. The statistics used for these observed trends have a lag time of about two years; therefore, the models using the trends also reflect two-year-old statistics. In addition, the overall historic trends average out the short-term fluctuations in activity levels of Gulf of Mexico OCS operations. The models cannot fully adjust for short-term changes in the rates of activities. Projecting short-term changes into the long term should not occur. Two examples of short-term change, technological advancements in seismic surveying and the enactment of the Deep Water Royalty Relief Act, contribute to the current resurgence of OCS activities in the Gulf. Increased levels of activity greater than the activity level predicted by the resources and socioeconomic models would be short-term effects. The acceleration of leasing and exploration cannot continue indefinitely. The MMS believes that the models, with continuing adjustments and refinements, adequately project Gulf OCS activities in the long term for the EIS analyses. The development scenarios do not represent an MMS recommendation, preference, or endorsement of any level of leasing or offshore operations, or of the types, numbers, and/or locations of any onshore operations or facilities.

Estimates of total reserve/resource production related to the proposed actions plus past and future sales (OCS Program) over the period 1998-2036 are 10.81 to 15.23 BBO and 122.23 to 170.41 tcf of gas. Estimates of total reserve/resource production related to the proposed actions plus prior and future sales (OCS Program) in the planning area over the period 1998-2036 are 9.25 to 12.35 BBO and 82.65 to 113.48 tcf of gas. This represents approximately 83 percent of the oil and 67 percent of the gas of the total Federal OCS Program.

As discussed in the CPA multisale EIS, the pace of exploration and development of oil and natural gas in the deepwater (water depths greater than 1,000 ft) Gulf of Mexico has accelerated rapidly in the last few years. In water depths exceeding 1,000 ft, the use of conventional, bottom-founded (fixed) platforms quickly becomes uneconomic. As industry makes new discoveries in deeper and deeper water, the innovative technologies used by industry continue to evolve to meet technical and economic needs for deepwater development. In most cases, production activities in deepwater and shelf development use similar technology and techniques. Deep water adds a level of complexity to the project, particularly subsea developments and completions, because the lessees may locate facilities remote from the control (host) facility and are not readily accessible. As part of an overall deepwater strategy, MMS prepared an EA (USDOI, MMS, 2000) for operations in the deepwater areas of the Gulf of Mexico OCS and on associated support activities and infrastructure. The Deepwater EA found that deepwater operations and activities do not substantially differ from those associated with conventional operations and activities on the continental shelf and that a programmatic EIS on regional deepwater activities on the Gulf of Mexico OCS is not required.

However, MMS found some activities substantially different and addressed them by preparing NEPA documents that identified and evaluated the potential impacts from operations in deep water and developed appropriate mitigation measures as needed. The NEPA documents being prepared and/or finalized by MMS addressed include

- modifying Notice to Lessees and Operators (NTL 2000-G20);
- initiated a Geological and Geophysical EA for the deep water; and
- preparing an EIS addressing floating production, storage, and offloading systems.

With regard to mitigating measures, MMS modified a Notice to Lessees and Operators (NTL 2000-G20) to include a 1,500-ft buffer zone around all deepwater well sites in order to avoid potentially significant impacts from drilling discharges on high-density chemosynthetic communities.

Deepwater seismic surveying operations do not essentially differ from seismic surveying operations on the continental shelf. However, the technology used for high-energy geophysical surveys has evolved in the past several years and make the potential impacts of the newer sound systems controversial. The MMS therefore initiated a separate EA to analyze geological and geophysical activities, including seismic surveying operations on the Gulf of Mexico OCS. The EA should be completed in early 2002.

The MMS also prepared an EIS addressing the possible environmental effects of the use of floating production, storage, and offloading systems (FPSO's). Major issues analyzed in the EIS include the storage of large volumes of crude oil offshore, potential emissions and spills associated with oil transfer operations, disposition of associated natural gas, and risks associated with shuttle tankering of OCS oil. The MMS completed the Final EIS January 2001. This EIS, a programmatic document, examined the concept of and fundamental issues associated with the petroleum industry's proposed use of FPSO in the deepwater areas of the Central and Western Planning Areas of the Gulf OCS. Therefore, the document addressed the proposed action generically and does not constitute a review of any site-specific development proposal. The EIS examined three alternatives: (1) conceptual approval of FPSO's (implementation of a policy approving the concept of using FPSO's in deepwater areas of the Central and Western Planning Areas of the GOM; (2) conditional Approval of FPSO's with general restrictions or conditions (implementation of accepting the conceptual use of FPSO's in the deepwater areas of the Central and Western Planning Areas of the GOM with certain restrictions); or (3) no action (i.e., no conceptual approval by the MMS at this time). The Record of Decision that is the culmination of this NEPA/EIS process is pending. Any FPSO's proposal will still be subject to established site-specific NEPA analysis and documentation.

B. UPDATE OF INFORMATION ON THE AFFECTED ENVIRONMENT

The Final EIS for CPA Sales 169, 172, 175, 178, and 182 (USDOI, MMS, 1997) provides a complete description of the affected environment for the proposed Central Gulf of Mexico lease sales. For a number of resources (geology; meteorology; water quality; coastal barrier beaches and associated dunes; wetlands; deepwater benthic communities; topographic features; marine mammals including sperm whales; Alabama, Choctawhatchee, and Perdido Key beach mice; sea turtles; coastal and marine birds; fish resources; Gulf sturgeon; public services, infrastructure, and land use plans; sociocultural issues and environmental justice; commercial fisheries; recreational resources and beach use; archaeological resources; and coastal zone management plans), MMS has identified no new significant information or issues since completion of the Final EIS. The reader should refer to the above-referenced document for information regarding these resources.

The following description summarizes the affected environment for those resources for which we have new information unavailable during the preparation of the Final EIS, which included Sale 182. This includes information on air quality, socioeconomic impact (population, labor, and employment), essential fish habitat (EFH), and critical habitat designation for wintering piping plover. At the time the Final EIS was completed in November 1997, the requirement for the assessment of potential impacts to EFH was not yet in place; therefore, the Final EIS did not consider EFH under a separate heading in the document. The EFH consultation is now required (and was conducted in March 2001) with NMFS pursuant to Section 305(b)(2) of the Magnuson Stevenson Fishery Conservation and Management Act. However, the offshore marine habitats considered by NMFS to be of particular importance as EFH in the CPA (i.e., Live Bottoms (Pinnacle Trend), deepwater benthic communities, and topographic features) were thoroughly discussed and analyzed in the Final EIS. Mitigations that would be applied to Live Bottoms, deepwater benthic communities, and topographic features would apply to EFH. Potential impacts to essential [fish] habitats are also included in the commercial fisheries analysis. To ensure that EFH is clearly identified as a resource/issue in this EA, a separate discussion of EFH and its authorizing legislation has been added to this section, and a brief analysis has been included in Section IV.C. below.

The most recent MMS sale, Central Gulf of Mexico Sale 178 (March 2001), received 780 bids on 547 tracts. Central Gulf of Mexico Sale 175 (March 2000) received 469 bids on 344 tracts. Central Gulf Sale 172 (March 1999) only received 272 bids on 207 tracts. The increase in bids reflects the gradually positive attitude toward the offshore oil and gas industry and a continued interest in the Gulf of Mexico, particularly in deepwater. Approximately 28 percent of the tracts receiving bids in Sale 178 were in ultra-deep water (more than 800 m).

Air Quality

Operations west of 87.5°W. longitude, which includes the entire CPA, fall under MMS jurisdiction for enforcement of the Clean Air Act; operations to the east are subject to U.S. Environmental Protection Agency (USEPA) air quality regulations.

The Clean Air Act Amendments of 1990 established classification designations based on regional monitored levels of ambient air quality. These designations impose mandated timetables and other requirements necessary for attaining and maintaining healthful air quality in the U.S. based on the seriousness of the regional air quality problem. When measured concentrations of regulated pollutants exceed standards established by the National Ambient Air Quality Standards (NAAQS), an area may be designated as a nonattainment area for a regulated pollutant. The number of exceedances and the concentrations determine the nonattainment classification of an area. The Clean Air Act Amendments of 1990 establish five classifications of nonattainment status: marginal, moderate, serious, severe, and extreme.

The USEPA does not classify the air over the OCS water for attainment status, but MMS presumes it to be better than the NAAQS for all criteria pollutants. Modeling of pollutant plumes indicate that there are areas where elevated levels of pollutants are moved offshore from coastal nonattainment areas. Gulf coastal counties and parishes currently contain areas both attaining and not attaining the NAAQS for ozone (Figure 2); the NAAQS for the remaining criteria pollutants are met in all of the coastal areas. Current O_3 nonattainment areas include the parishes of Ascension, East Baton Rouge, West Baton Rouge, Iberville, Livingston, and LaFourche in Louisiana and the counties of Hardin, Jefferson, Orange, Brazoria, Chambers, Fort Bend, Galveston, Harris, Liberty, Montgomery, and Waller in Texas. This new information, formalized after November 1997, will not change the analysis or the expected impacts to air quality previously discussed in the Final EIS and has not been carried forward for further analysis. The Breton National Wilderness Area (Figure 3), south of Mississippi and northeast of the Mississippi Delta, is a prevention of significant deterioration (PSD) Class I Area. Class I Areas are afforded the greatest degree of air quality protection. Very little deterioration of air quality is allowed in these areas. One of the purposes of the PSD program is to preserve, protect, and enhance the air quality in these designated areas.

Socioeconomic Impact Area

Population, Labor, and Employment

The MMS defines the Gulf of Mexico impact area for population, labor, and employment as that portion of the Gulf of Mexico coastal zone whose social and economic well-being (population, labor, and employment) is directly or indirectly affected by the OCS oil and gas industry. For this analysis, the coastal impact area consists of 51 counties and parishes in the Central and Western Gulf of Mexico. Inland counties and parishes are included where offshore oil and gas activities are known to exist, where offshore-related petroleum industries are established, and where one or more counties or parishes within a Metropolitan Statistical Area (MSA) are on the coast; all counties and parishes within the MSA are included. The counties and parishes in the impact area are classified in two planning areas: the CPA and the WPA. While most of the economic impacts from a Central Gulf of Mexico sale, about 75 percent, are projected to occur in the CPA, there are some employment, population, and labor implications associated with economic communities in the WPA, especially along the eastern Texas coastal areas.

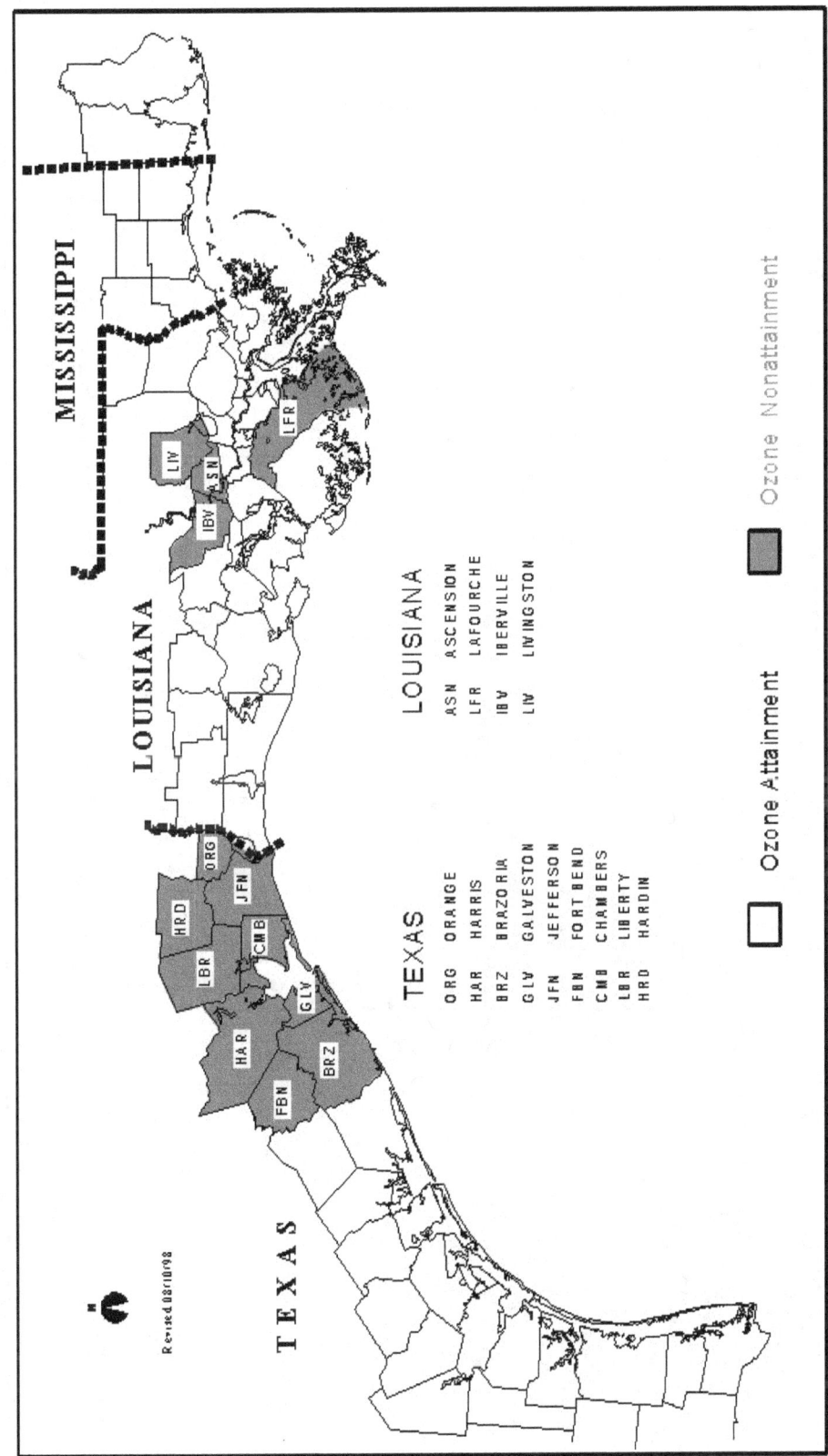

Figure 2. Status of Ozone Attainment in the Coastal Counties and Parishes of the Central and Western Gulf of Mexico (based on the NAAQS effective 8/10/98).

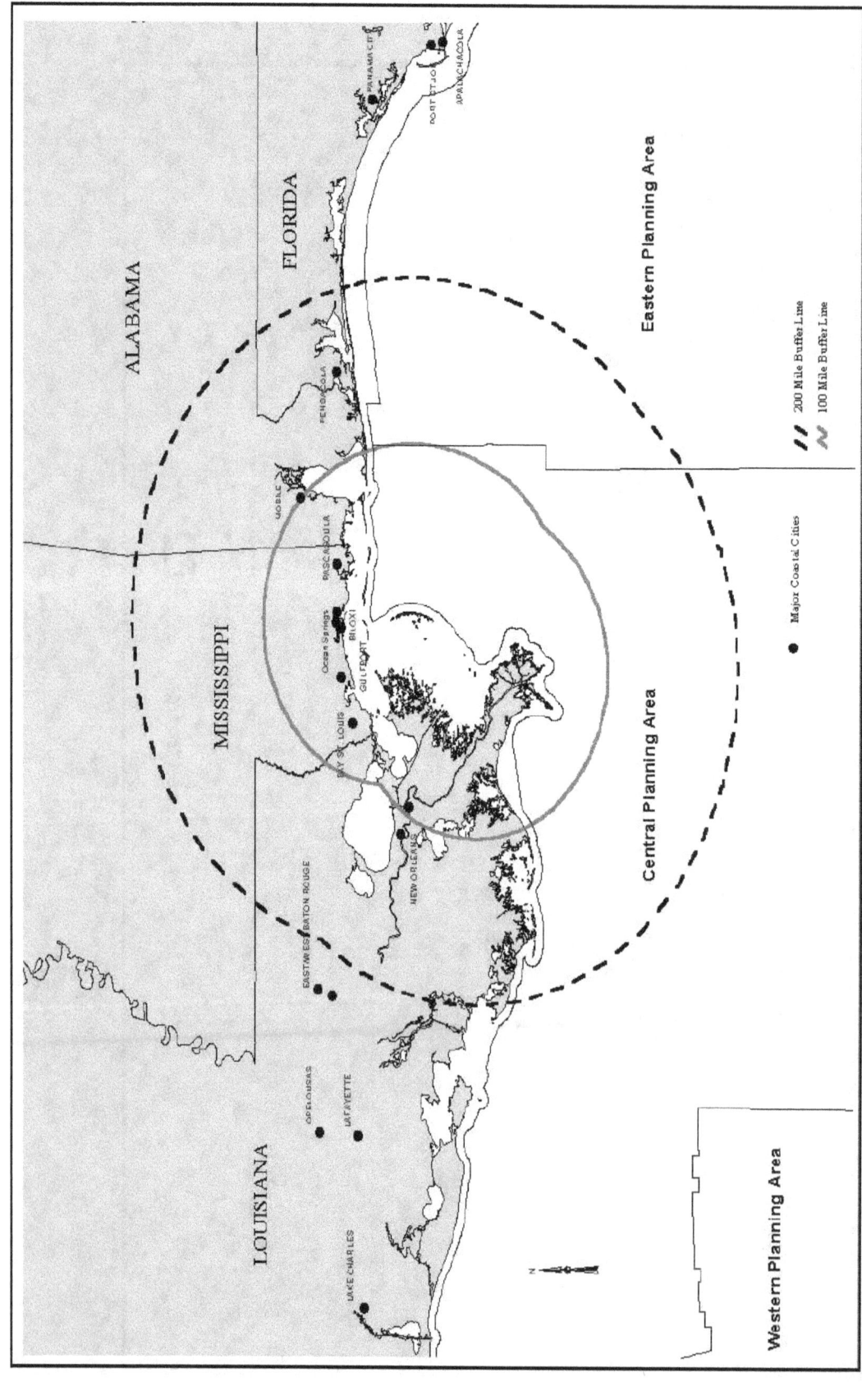

Figure 3. Breton National Wilderness Area.

The Central and Western Gulf region impact area includes the following 14 MSA's:

Central Gulf of Mexico

Alabama	Mobile
Louisiana	Baton Rouge
	Houma
	Lafayette
	Lake Charles
	New Orleans
Mississippi	Biloxi-Gulfport-Pascagoula

Western Gulf of Mexico

Texas	Beaumont-Port Arthur
	Brazoria
	Brownsville-Harlingen-San Benito
	Corpus Christi
	Galveston-Texas City
	Houston
	Victoria

As of 1997 the most populated MSA's are Houston, Texas, and New Orleans, Louisiana. The least populated MSA's are Lake Charles, Louisiana, and Victoria, Texas. During the time period of 1994-1997, Brownsville-Harlingen-San Benito experienced the largest, positive population growth rate (7.4%), while Houston's 200,000 population growth was the largest in numerical terms. New Orleans remained unchanged (Woods and Poole Economics, Inc., 1999).

How OCS Development Has Affected the Impact Area

1980 — 1989

In the oil and gas industry, drilling rig use is employed as a barometer of economic activity. Between the end of 1981 and mid-1983 drilling rig activity in the Gulf of Mexico took a sharp downturn. By 1986 the demand for mobile drilling rigs had suffered an even greater decline. Population and net migration paralleled these fluctuations in mobile drilling rig activity. Population growth rates for all coastal subareas were relatively high prior to 1983; families moved to the Gulf looking for work in the booming oil and gas industry. Lower rates of population growth accompanied the decline in drilling activity as workers were laid off and left the area in search of work elsewhere. After 1983, all subareas experienced several years of significant net migration out of the region. The negative impact on population continued until 1986 when the demand for mobile rigs declined to its lowest level in over a decade and the price of oil collapsed.

1990 — 1997

In the early to mid-1990's, the impact area experienced a major resurgence in oil exploration and drilling due to advances in technology and the enactment of the Deep Water Royalty Relief Act in 1995. The renewed interest in oil and gas exploration and development in the Gulf of Mexico produced a modest to significant recovery from the high unemployment levels experienced after the 1986 downturn. Ironically, the Gulf Coast encountered a shortage of skilled labor in the oil and gas industry due to the restructuring of the oil industry to centralize management, finance and business services, and the use of computer technology, (Baxter, 1990). Additionally, potential oil and gas industry employees experienced the shadow effect. Workers who previously lost high-paying jobs in the oil industry (or oil service industry) during the 1980s downturn were reluctant to return. The shadow effect, coupled with the shortage of skilled labor where the core problems were lack of education and or training for requisite skills, created a situation where temporary communities of workers from out of the area (some from out of the country) were established. Furthermore, the higher skill levels required by deepwater development drilling could not be completely met by the existing impact area's labor force causing in-migration. Unemployment in the impact area, though, declined due to increased economic diversification by the region.

1998 — Present

In early 1998 crude oil prices were hovering near 12-year lows. This restrained the resurgence of exploration and development activity in the Gulf of Mexico. While offshore development strategy varies by company, most major oil companies, diversified firms, and small independents cut back production and curtailed exploration projects. Several large integrated companies resorted to layoffs and mergers as ways to assail low prices; a redistribution of headquarter personnel from the New Orleans area to the Houston area occurred and unemployment in the impact area rose. Offshore drilling strategies focused on mega and large prospects, foregoing small prospects, and only considered medium prospects when prices rose (Rike, 1998). A few companies, though, took advantage of lower drilling rates during this period and increased their drilling. Concurrently, technological innovations (such as 3-D seismic, slim hole drilling, and hydraulic rigs) decreased the cost of extraction and thus stimulated the development of large or mega prospects that were still considered economic at low prices

In March 1999, OPEC, which produces 40 percent of the world's oil, announced crude oil production cutbacks. Full member compliance increased oil prices to 20-year highs encouraging moderate exploration and development spending during the 1999 fiscal year. Crude oil prices continued to increase during 2000 and now into 2001. It is generally believed that the increase in price is being driven by two major factors. The first factor is the continued OPEC compliance to maintain prices within their current output targets of a $22 minimum and a $28 maximum barrel price. This was recently fortified by the cartel's January 17, 2001, announcement to cut production by 1.5 million barrels per day beginning February 1, 2001, in order to increase the price. The second factor, according to the Federal Reserve Bank of Dallas, is the "world capacity to supply oil has not kept pace with the growth of oil demand spurred by a resurgent world economy. Furthermore a short supply of oil tankers, rising shipping rates and low inventories of refined product and crude oil have added upward pressure to spot crude oil prices." (Brown, 2000). The low prices throughout much of the 1990's were too low to stimulate additions to capacity. In addition, many tankers were scrapped in the 1990's when weak demand, low shipping rates and increasing environmental regulation put a lot of pressure on the tanker industry (Brown, 2000). High oil prices and Federal environmental clean air efforts have prompted fuel switching away from crude oil to natural gas. Like crude oil, supply of natural gas did not keep up with demand, pushing prices higher. In December 2000, natural gas broke record highs, closing at $10.10. Matthew Simmons, industry analyst and president of Houston investment bank Simmons & Co., states, "in addition to heating about 53 percent of American homes, natural gas is also being used to generate about 16 percent of the country's electricity — a percentage that is still growing." (Simmons, 2001). Mr. Simmons believes, and many other analysts concur, that this is "a decade-long problem" (Simmons, 2001). However, in recent months, natural gas prices have decreased dramatically (75.25%) since its record high of $10.10. According to Kelley Doolan, a natural gas market specialist for Platts and chief editor of Inside FERC's Gas Market Report, several factors have kept a downward pressure on natural prices in recent months. These factors include moderate weather conditions in most of the nation, which kept the demand for natural gas by electricity generators in check; relatively low oil prices; and the general economic slowdown, which has reduced demand for gas by the industrial sector. Even without this pronounced drop in price, demand growth for natural gas is expected to be strong during the next 20 years. The American Gas Association in their 2001 Update of the Fueling the Future: Natural Gas and New Technologies for a Cleaner 21st Century report projects that natural gas demand would increase by 53 percent by the year 2020.

Current Economic Baseline Data

Current crude oil and natural gas prices are substantially above the economically viable threshold for drilling in the Gulf of Mexico. As of September 7, 2001, Light Sweet Crude lists for $28.03 per barrel on the New York Mercantile Exchange (a decrease of 7.22% or $2.18 from a year ago). Henry Hub Natural Gas closed at $2.50 per million BTU (a decrease of 35.73% or $1.39 from a year ago) (www.oilnergy.com). In addition to oil and gas prices, drilling rig use is employed by the industry as a barometer of economic activity. According to Offshore Data Services, the utilization rate for all marketed mobile rigs in the Gulf of Mexico was 78.4 percent. This breaks down as a 72.9 percent utilization rate for jackups (average day rates of $26,000-66,000); 91.7 percent for semisubmersibles (average day rates of $45,000-135,000); 100 percent for drillships (average day rates of $125,000-150,000); and 100 percent for submersibles (average day rates of $35,00-43,000). Platform rigs in the Gulf recorded a 71.9 percent utilization rate, while inland barges had a 92 percent utilization rate (Offshore Data Services, 2001).

Offshore service vessel (OSV) day rates, another indicator of the industry's activity, remains strong despite the softening of the drilling rig market, which most vessel operators believe will become active later this year (*WorkBoat*, 2001). The July 2001 average day rates for all three types of vessels used by the offshore oil and gas industry increased from the July 2000 averages. Anchor-handling tug/supply vessel (AHTS) average day rates ranged from $10,500 for under 6,000-hp vessels to $12,500 for over 6,000-hp vessels; utilization rates were 88 percent and 100 percent, respectively. Supply boat average day rates ranged from $7,718 for boats up to 200 ft and $10,950 for 200 ft and over; utilization was 89 percent and 100 percent, respectively. Crewboat average day rates ranged from $2,928 for boats under 125 ft to $3,775 for boats 125 ft and over; utilization was 100 percent and 98 percent, respectively. Another indicator of the direction of the industry is the exploration and development (E&D) expenditures of the major oil and gas companies. After substantially cutting their E&D budgets during the 1998 and 1999 fiscal years, majors are once again increasing these areas on their balance sheets. According to Global Marine Chairman, President, and CEO, Bob Rose, ". . .the outlook for 2001 is very bullish." (Rose, 2001).

Commencing with Central Gulf of Mexico Lease Sale 178 Part 1 in March 2001, new royalty relief provisions for both oil and gas production in the Gulf of Mexico's deep and shallow waters were implemented. These rules will govern the next three years of lease sales. Central Gulf Lease Sale 178 Part 1 resulted in 534 leases (an increase of 59.88% or 200 blocks from Central Gulf Lease Sale 175 in March 2000). Of these 534 leases, 348 are in shallow water (0-400 m). This increase of 67.30 percent from the last Central Gulf lease sale largely reflects the intensified interest in natural gas due to higher prices over the last year and the new royalty relief provisions. The 186 blocks receiving bids in deepwater (greater than 400 m) reflects an increase of 47.62 percent or 60 blocks. Again, this dramatic increase in leasing could be a result of the recently issued royalty relief provisions. Western Gulf of Mexico Lease Sale 180 and Central Gulf of Mexico Lease Sale 178 Part 2, offering the newly available United States' blocks beyond the U.S. Exclusive Economic Zone, were held on August 22, 2001. No bids were received for blocks offered in Central Gulf Lease Sale 178 Part 2. Of the 4,114 blocks offered in Western Gulf Lease Sale 180, 320 received bids. About 55 percent of the blocks receiving bids (or 177 blocks) in Lease Sale 180 are in deepwater (water depths greater than 1,000 ft [305 m]).

According to Woods and Poole 1998 economic data, the most recent data available, Houston, Texas, and New Orleans, Louisiana, remain the largest populated MSA's in the impact area. The least populated MSA's remain Lake Charles, Louisiana, and Victoria, Texas. During the time period of 1997-1998, the Biloxi-Gulf Port-Pascagoula MSA experienced the largest, positive population growth rate, 0.25 percent, while Houston's loss in population of 4,650 was the largest in numerical terms. This current data though does not reflect the oil and gas industry's consolidation to Houston over the last two years. Woods and Poole forecast the Houston MSA will grow at a rate of 6.8 percent over the 1998-2001 period or a change of 261,730 people. Despite the industry's exodus to Houston, the population in the New Orleans MSA is forecasted to grow 1.29 percent (Woods and Poole Economics, Inc., 1999).

Based on the economic activity in the Gulf of Mexico OCS Region, MMS estimates that about 48,200 jobs are directly dependent on the offshore oil and gas program as of June 2001. This is an increase of almost 8,400 jobs (or about 21%) from a year ago, reflecting the rise in exploration and production activity over the last year.

In light of the September 11, 2001, terrorist attacks on the United States, oil prices have surged, as oil and gold typically do with international tension. With the attacks possibly linked to recent instability in the Middle East and while the world waited for a United States' response, U.S. traders expected oil price increases. However, the Secretary-General of OPEC, Ali Rodriguez, said that the Arab-dominated cartel would ensure world oil supplies and price stability (COMTEX, 2001).

How OCS Development is Currently Affecting the Impact Area

In June 2001, MMS received 43 letters from Lafourche Parish, Louisiana, government representatives, businesses, and citizens in response to MMS's request for comments on the Environmental Assessment for Proposed OCS Lease Sale 182, Central Gulf of Mexico, published in the *Federal Register* on May 21, 2001. These letters are summarized in Appendix A of this EA and highlight Port Fourchon as unusually important to the OCS oil industry, particularly to deepwater activities. The respondents stressed their concern for the onshore impacts of the OCS program on the local infrastructure, in particular the effects on LA Highway 1 and the Lafourche Parish water supply. In response to these letters, the Associate Director of Offshore Minerals Management and the Regional Director of the Gulf of Mexico OCS Region, along with other MMS representatives, met with government and industry representatives of Port Fourchon and Lockport, Louisiana, to discuss their concerns of OCS onshore impacts. The Lafourche Parish Water District No. 1 is located in Lockport. A full account of this trip is contained in Appendix B of this document. Information attained at these meetings is incorporated into the discussion below.

The EIS that covers proposed Lease Sale 182 (USDOI, MMS, 1997) stated that, while the level of OCS-related employment expected to result from the proposed action in the Central Gulf is not significant, some employment would be met through in-migration due to the shadow effect and a labor force lacking requisite skills for the oil and gas and supporting industries. The presence of some in-migrants has been reported for south Lafourche Parish, including workers from Mexico and India. This temporary importation of labor, particularly in the South Lafourche area of Louisiana, is expected to continue in the near future. This is a unique situation exacerbated by the shadow effect. The unusual work schedules in the oil and gas extraction industry also supports employment outside the impact area, since long-distance commuting can be reasonably accomplished on such an infrequent basis. So while employment opportunities are growing in the oil and gas extraction and supporting industries within the Gulf of Mexico impact area, some of that employment will be met from outside the area. Large, short-term increases in the workforce could result in net positive migration and cause a scarcity of housing, a shortage of municipal personnel (i.e., policemen, firemen, engineers, etc.), stresses on the capabilities of available infrastructure, and an increase in the cost of living. Edison Chouest Offshore, which owns C-Port and C-Port 2 in Port Fourchon, North American Shipbuilding in Larose, Louisiana, and North American Fabricators in Houma, Louisiana, has experienced these impacts first hand. Unable to find housing for their workers, Chouest built an apartment complex for the workers they had to recruit from outside of Louisiana due to the labor and skills shortage within the state.

Recent technological advances and the passage of the Deep Water Royalty Relief Act in 1995 have stimulated deepwater leasing and subsequent exploration and development activities beyond expectations. The models used to predict employment associated with a typical proposed action take the larger and more complex nature of these operations into account. However, as stated in the November 1997 EIS, needs specific to these deepwater projects may result in more focused stresses placed on areas that are capable of supporting these large-scale development projects (e.g., ports that can handle deeper draft service vessels such as Port Fourchon, Louisiana). This focusing of activity could result in stresses to infrastructure servicing these focal points (particularly highways and ports), as well as stresses placed on the infrastructure associated with the focal point. This is what is occurring at Port Fourchon.

Port Fourchon is one of the Gulf of Mexico's main service bases for OCS activities, especially for deepwater services. While the port has maintained steady growth over the last 25 years, the rise of deepwater exploration has produced rapid growth at the port in the last 5 years, causing the port to become one of the OCS program's focal points. At present, there are over 120 businesses at Port Fourchon, most of which are oil and gas in nature. Over 82,500 offshore workers per year go through the port to offshore by helicopter, while 200 vessels a day travel in and out of the port (from monthly helicopter logs). As the port has grown, its importance to the U.S.'s energy infrastructure has increased significantly. According to the Executive Director of Port Fourchon, Mr. Ted Falgout, the port has a 20 percent interest/influence on U.S. oil and gas. This number was calculated based on the fact that 20 percent of the Nation's oil and 25-27 percent of the natural gas is located offshore Louisiana. In addition, the port plays some role in 90 percent of the deepwater and 68 percent of the shallow-water offshore oil and gas activities, resulting in the port being involved in 75 percent of the total offshore oil and gas volumes. Lastly, 85 percent of the 200 vessels that go into and out of the port each day are OCS-related (from daily port logs of vessels in port). These numbers are supported by the port's servicing of offshore mobile rigs. As of September 5, 2001, Port Fourchon is servicing about 39 percent of all offshore mobile rigs working in the Gulf of Mexico OCS. Of this total, nearly 59 percent are located in deepwater (Offshore Data Services, 2001). Furthermore, the Louisiana Offshore Oil Port (LOOP), which is located 18 mi off Port Fourchon and which has offices at the port, transports 13-15 percent of imported foreign crude oil. LOOP is also connected to 30 percent of the U.S. refineries. At present, floating production, storage, and offloading systems (FPSO's) have not been approved by MMS for operation in the Gulf of Mexico. However, with the increasing importance of deepwater development and the potential for FPSO's working in the Gulf of Mexico in the near future, LOOP will become even more important to the U.S.'s energy intermodal system and, therefore, so will Port Fourchon.

Unlike the ports of Iberia or Morgan City, Louisiana, Port Fourchon is not a manufacturing port, but an intermodal transfer port — a service/supply base. There are numerous oil and gas service companies located at the port. BP and Shell are based from the port. All three major helicopter companies (ERA, PHI, and Air Logistics) have heliports at the port. ERA is currently building a $4 million new, larger heliport at the port, which will be completed in 2002. Air Logistics is planning to build a similar facility. LOOP, who has offices at the port, is also expanding its storage volumes with three large aboveground tanks in Galliano, Louisiana. Halliburton, another port tenant, recently completed a state-of-the-art drilling liquids facility at C-Port. Chevron and Texaco have tank farms at the port, while there are seven ship and barge repair facilities located at the port. In addition, the port has five barge lines and six barge fleeting operations.

In 1996 Edison Chouest built its highly successful C-Port at Port Fourchon. The C-Port is a multi-services port terminal facility supplying offshore vessels that operate in the Gulf of Mexico. The C-Port can load/offload deck cargoes, fuel, water, cements, barites, liquid muds, and completion fuels simultaneously. These services are provided under the protection of a covered building, eliminating weather and darkness, while improving safety and efficiency, making it a highly cost-effective, cost-saving solution (http://www.chouest.com/C-Port/c-port.html). According to Roger White, Vice President of Business Development for Edison Chouest Offshore, prior to C-Port, it took 2-3 days to service a vessel. Today service time is down to a few hours. This results in huge dollar savings for offshore companies. In addition, the companies need to lease fewer service boats because of the larger, technologically advanced ships that Chouest is building. In 1999 Chouest completed a second C-Port at Port Fourchon, C-Port 2. The company is currently adding three more slips to C-Port 2. Together C-Port and C-Port 2 are servicing 90 percent of deepwater activity. In addition to the port expansion, Chouest began an aggressive new building program in the late 1990's for their offshore service vessels. The company has produced over 50 new generation offshore vessels to serve deepwater oil and gas production. The new vessels are larger (260 ft) and faster than their predecessors that service shallow-water activities. The C-Ports and the new deepwater service vessels have increased activity at Port Fourchon exponentially.

Only a few ports in the Gulf of Mexico (including Port Fourchon) can accommodate these larger ships that now service OCS deepwater, according to Mr. White. Morgan City and Iberia, Louisiana, lack the necessary channel depth for servicing deepwater. Lake Charles and Venice, Louisiana, have the channel depth, but are farther inland than Port Fourchon. In addition, Venice has problems with fog on the Mississippi River and with large ship and tanker traffic. Based on OCS activity at the port, the Corps of Engineers (COE) justified deepening Port Fourchon's channel from 12 ft to 24 ft. The port had been maintaining the channel at 20 ft for the larger OCS supply vessels. In August 2001 the COE began dredging the channel to a depth of 26 ft (24 ft plus 2 ft of advance maintenance) and will maintain this depth in the future.

The limited number of service bases capable of servicing deepwater activities suggests that stresses placed on local infrastructure at these bases will continue as a result of the typical proposed action to the extent that deepwater tracts are leased, explored, and developed. Recent leasing history has shown an increase in deepwater interest. The MMS's Gulf of Mexico OCS Region sponsored a workshop in April 1997 to identify information needs related to deepwater environmental resources and potential impacts of deepwater activities, including socioeconomic impacts. Information needs identified in the socioeconomic session of the workshop included an infrastructure inventory of the Gulf Region and identification of stresses on the infrastructure resulting from deepwater activity; an examination of port facilities across the Gulf; and an examination of employment and commuting patterns. The MMS-funded studies to examine these deepwater impacts are currently underway and/or recently completed. The MMS is sponsoring a follow-up workshop related to deepwater issues in June 2002.

LA Highway 1 (LA 1) is the main land-based mode of transportation to and from the port, making it vital to the U.S.'s energy infrastructure. According to Roy Francis, Executive Director of the LA 1 Coalition, the highway is currently substandard and will not be able to handle the increased traffic associated with OCS activities. The deterioration of the road is extensive due to coastal landloss from wave forces; LA 1 divides the Barataria and Terrebonne estuaries. While Port Fourchon has been active in building up the embankment with channel dredging materials, it is a short-term fix to a long-term problem that grows worse every day. At present, Golden Meadow to Larose is the only section of the highway that is four lanes. The State of Louisiana (Department of Transportation) and the port are completing an EIS on the section from Golden Meadow to Port Fourchon, while a corridor study on the section from Larose to U.S. 90 is finished. Funding for the new highway is estimated at $500 million; the State, which controls LA 1, does not have the money according to Mr. Roy Francis.

Results from an MMS-funded study on the infrastructural impacts of expanding OCS oil and gas activities in south Lafourche Parish indicate the levels of service provided by LA 1 will decline significantly through time. The study estimated a 3 percent low-case growth in daily vehicle traffic along LA 1 and a 6 percent high-case growth. Based on traffic count data by the port, actual 2000 vehicle growth was 24 percent while 2001 vehicle growth is 13 percent. The increasing significance of deepwater drilling primarily serviced by Port Fourchon serves to intensify this trend. The study also confirms that deterioration of LA 1 will be exacerbated with expanding oil and gas activities, particularly those in deepwater (Guo et al., 2000). The size and complexity of these deepwater projects, along with the limited number of service bases capable of handling their unique needs, and the addition of the new Edison Chouest Offshore C-Port (in 1996) and C-Port 2 (in 1999) at Port Fourchon, will likely result in continued stresses on port infrastructure and associated stresses placed on the local infrastructure, especially LA 1 and the parish's and water supply. Chouest has started building a C-Port at Galveston to service deepwater activities in the Western Gulf and is looking into locations in Mississippi and Alabama to build a C-Port to service deepwater activities in the Eastern Gulf. Several other service bases have recently seen a large increase in OCS-related activity and concomitant stresses placed on their local infrastructure. These ports include Cameron, Venice, and Morgan City, Louisiana, which are servicing 18 percent, 15 percent, and 10 percent of OCS-related offshore mobile rig activity respectively (Offshore Data Services, 2001).

The quality of life in the local Lafourche Parish community has decreased due to LA 1 traffic. According to the LA 1 Coalition, which was created in 1997 to help Lafourche Parish receive funding for a new four-lane highway from U.S. 90 to Port Fourchon, LA 1 is twice as deadly as any similar class highway in the United States. The number of fatalities on LA 1 has increased directly with the growth of OCS activity and, therefore, the port. Exacerbating the traffic problems associated with LA 1 are the delays caused by bridge openings to accommodate barge traffic. Port Fourchon officials estimate that 50 percent of all oil and gas materials brought to the port is barged down Bayou Lafourche. This means that each of the parish's six bridges must open for each barge that goes to and from the port. On average, each bridge is opened 16 times a day (from Port Fourchon tonnage report logs), resulting in impacts to the communities along LA 1 — long waits in traffic, missed appointments, increased number of accidents, flaring emotions, and a lower quality of life. The Leeville Bridge, when it breaks down or there is an accident, can impasse traffic for several hours. Considering there are an estimated 6,000 cars that need to be evacuated from Port Fourchon during a storm, the potential for disaster is high (from Port Fourchon inventory of vehicles).

Part of the increased barge traffic along Bayou Lafourche results from shipping freshwater to Port Fourchon for offshore activities. Deepwater expansion has increased the demand for water, taxing the local freshwater district. The Lafourche Parish Water District No. 1, which is located in Lockport, services Port Fourchon. Despite $10 million in improvements from Lockport to Golden Meadow, the water district is currently at maximum capacity. Port Fourchon uses 30 percent of the Lockport plant's water supply, but only comprises 1 percent of the serving population (from the Water District). The differential comes from the offshore demand that the port is servicing. Water consumption for the Lockport water district increased 20 percent in 2000. The water plant was able to accommodate this increase in demand because Grand Isle no longer needed service from the Lockport plant. In 1999/2000, Grand Isle received its own water line from Jefferson Parish. It is estimated that the water district's consumption will increase 4 percent in 2001. The water district is not expected to be able to meet this demand despite issuing a second $10 million bond for improvements for a new larger line from Golden Meadow to Port Fourchon.

Port Fourchon has become a focal stress point. The port believes that an investment in a new highway is an investment in a Federal resource; it is an energy security argument. Port Fourchon by its nature affects the domestic supply (GOM OCS) and foreign supply (LOOP) of oil and gas. Mr. Falgout, Executive Director of Port Fourchon, stressed that if a storm came through and destroyed the local infrastructure, in particular LA 1, the price of oil and gas would increase due to the decrease in supply. In addition, in a storm, more than 3,000 offshore workers, 1,000 port personnel, and 5,000 citizens from Grand Isle and Leeville (south of the bridge) must evacuate the area by LA 1. Furthermore, offshore companies take valuable equipment, such as bagged drilling fluids, off the rigs and bring it to safety inland. This increases the truck traffic along LA 1 during the evacuation process.

Louisiana representatives are pushing for the approval of the Conservation and Reinvestment Act (CARA), a permanent revenue-sharing program for coastal states affected by Federal offshore oil and gas leases, which will mitigate impacts from offshore oil and gas development. Because CARA monies are to be used for all impacts from offshore oil and gas development and only a portion can go to infrastructure such as highways, Port Fourchon officials do not feel that CARA is the complete answer to the LA 1 problems. While CARA did not get congressional approval in 2000 (it passed in the House of Representatives and failed in the Senate), the Coastal Impact Assistance Program (CIAP), a one-time $150 million Federal allocation to seven oil- and gas-producing states, was authorized by Congress to assist states in mitigating the impacts from OCS oil and gas production. CIAP allocated $26.4 million to Louisiana. Terrebonne and Lafourche Parishes received about 30 percent of that amount. However, only 23 percent ($6 million) of CIAP monies can be used for infrastructure projects, such as roads and bridges. About half of that went to Lafourche Parish for infrastructure, most of which will fund a study on the proposed Leon Theriot Lock south of Golden Meadow. Supporters of a proposed elevated four-lane highway to and from Port Fourchon have pushed to replace the Leeville Bridge with an overpass. Federal money for the proposed overpass will pay for engineering and design work (*The Courier Houma Today*, 2001). CARA is again being considered in Congress. Should it be authorized, Louisiana would receive more than $293 million in oil and gas royalties and "coastal impact" assistance from all drilling activities within 200 mi of its shoreline (The Courier Houma Today, 2001a). The version, approved by the Senate Energy Committee, is less generous to oil-producing states such as Louisiana. It would provide the state with about $170 million a year (*The Times-Picayune*, 2001). CARA funds are for the mitigation of all OCS impacts both statewide and parish/county specific, are prioritized on the State level, and are approved by the National Oceanic and Atmospheric Administration (NOAA), the Federal agency that administers CARA. However, Port Fourchon officials do not believe that CARA will completely resolve the LA 1 problems.

Fishery Conservation and Management Act

In 1996 Congress, recognizing the importance of fish habitat to the productivity and sustainability of U.S. marine fisheries, added habitat conservation provisions to the Magnuson-Stevens Fishery Conservation and Management Act (FCMA) amended through October 11, 1996, 16 U.S.C. 1801-1883. This Act stated that the continuing loss of marine, estuarine, and other aquatic habitats is one of the greatest long-term threats to the viability of commercial and recreational fisheries. Habitat considerations should receive increased attention for the conservation and management of U.S. fish resources.

The FCMA directed that any fishery management plan (FMP) prepared by any Council or by the Secretary should describe and identify essential fish habitat (EFH) for fishery resources under its authority and minimize, to the extent practicable, the adverse effects on the habitat caused by fishing, as well as identify other actions to encourage the conservation and enhancement of such habitat. The EFH Interim Final Rule (50 CFR) defines EFH as the water and substrate necessary for fish spawning, breeding, feeding, or growth to maturity. The Act also requires that Federal agencies consult with the Secretary of Commerce on any action authorized, funded, or undertaken by any Federal or State agency that may affect the habitat, including EFH.

Essential Fish Habitat

There are FMP's in the GOM region for shrimp, red drum, reef fishes, coastal migratory pelagics, stone crabs, spiny lobsters, coral and coral reefs, and highly migratory species (HMS). While there were over 450 species identified in the original FMP's, information on habitat requirements was severely limited for many species. The Gulf of Mexico FMC Generic Amendment for Addressing Essential Fish Habitat Requirements amends the first seven FMP's listed above using 26 selected managed species and the coral complex. These species were chosen because they were ecologically representative of the remaining species within their respective Fishery Management Units and, in most cases, sufficient information was available to document and map their habitat associations and use. The EFH for 46 highly migratory species is designated in the U.S. Department of Commerce, National Marine Fisheries Service's (NMFS) Final Fishery Management Plan for Atlantic tunas, swordfish, and sharks (Volume II, April 1999). The EFH for many of the 46 species includes portions of the Gulf of Mexico.

Habitat Areas of Particular Concern

Within the EFH Interim Final Rule, the NMFS recommended that FMP's identify habitat areas of particular concern (HAPC) in EFH. The HAPC's include the following: (1) nearshore areas of intertidal and estuarine habitats with emergent and submerged vegetation, sand and mud flats, shell and oyster reefs, and other substrates that may provide food and rearing for juvenile fish and shellfish; migration routes for adult and juvenile fish and shellfish; and areas sensitive to human-induced developmental activities; (2) offshore areas with substrates of high habitat value and diversity or vertical relief that serve as cover for fish and shellfish; and (3) marine and estuarine habitat used for migration, spawning, and rearing of fish and shellfish, especially in areas adjacent to intensive human-induced developmental activities.

The Gulf of Mexico Fishery Management Council has designated nine HAPC's to date. All of these HAPC's are important with respect to corals and coral reefs and provide habitats for reef species such as snappers, groupers, and spiny lobster. The Flower Garden Banks National Marine Sanctuary is an example of one of the HAPC's.

Piping Plover Critical Habitat Designation

The piping plover (*Charadrius melodus*) is a migratory shorebird that is endemic to North America. The piping plover breeds on the northern Great Plains, in the Great Lakes, and along the Atlantic Coast (Newfoundland to North Carolina). It overwinters on the Atlantic and Gulf of Mexico coasts from North Carolina to Mexico and in the Bahamas West Indies. Hypothetically, plovers may have a preferred prey base and/or the substrate coloration provides protection from aerial predators due to chromatic matching camouflage in specific wintering habitat. Such areas include coastal sand flats and mud flats in proximity to large inlets or passes, which may attract the largest concentrations of piping plovers (Nicholls and Baldassarre, 1990). This species remains in a precarious state given its low population numbers, sparse distribution, and continued threats to habitat throughout its range.

Piping plover critical habitat in the Gulf of Mexico has been designated in Texas, Louisiana, Mississippi, Alabama, and Florida. The designation was published in the *Federal Register* on July 10, 2001, and became effective August 9, 2001. All piping plovers on their wintering grounds are considered threatened species under the Endangered Species Act of 1973, as amended.

Critical habitat identifies specific areas that are essential to the conservation of piping plover, and that may require special management considerations for the primary biological needs of foraging, sheltering, and roosting. These areas are called primary constituent elements and are found in coastal areas that support intertidal beaches and flats and associated dune systems and flats above high tide. Specific areas outside the geographic area occupied by a species at the time it is listed may be designated upon determination that such areas are essential for the conservation of the species.

C. IMPACTS FROM ALTERNATIVE A — THE PROPOSED ACTION

1. Summary of Analysis Incorporated by Reference from the Multisale EIS

The multisale EIS proposed action analyzed the effects of a typical Central Gulf of Mexico lease sale by presenting a set of ranges for resource estimates, projected exploration and development activities, and impact-producing factors for any of the proposed Central Gulf sales held over the five-year period. This EA tiers off the initial multisale EIS and incorporates that document by reference. All unleased blocks in the CPA will be available for lease under the proposed action, but MMS expects only a small percentage to be leased, and an even smaller percentage will actually produce oil and gas. A brief summary of impacts to resource categories is as follows.

Coastal Barrier Beaches and Wetlands: The MMS does not expect sale-related activities to result in permanent alterations of barrier beach configurations. Small spills from pipeline and navigation accidents may result in the conversion of small amounts of wetlands to open water.

Sensitive Offshore Resources: The MMS expects little damage to either low- or high-density chemosynthetic communities. Low-density communities are highly dispersed and widespread. High-density communities are protected by a requirement to search for their presence prior to drilling or platform placement. Little to no damage is expected to sensitive bathymetric features. Small areas would be impacted by operational discharges (muds and cuttings) or in the unlikely event of a seafloor blowout. Adoption of the Topographic Features Stipulation would provide for adequate protection to these areas.

Water Quality: Marine and coastal waters would be slightly degraded from discharges of drilling muds and because of greater turbidity from OCS support activities. Further degradation would occur from chronic, low-level contamination from produced-water discharges, site runoff, and maritime traffic activities.

Air Quality: Emissions from operational activities are expected to have minimum effects on offshore air quality. The MMS expects onshore impacts on air quality to be negligible because of prevailing atmospheric conditions, emission rates, and the distance of these emissions from shore. Onshore air quality classifications would not change as a result of these operations.

Marine Mammals, Fisheries, Turtles, and Birds: Exploration and development activities could impact fish and wildlife inhabiting either coastal or marine environments. Small numbers of marine mammals and sea turtles could be killed or injured by chance collision with service vessels and by eating indigestible trash, accidentally lost from drill rigs and service vessels. Although an interaction with a spill could occur and contaminants might indirectly affect marine mammals through their food supply, the proposed action is not expected to cause fatalities or have long-term adverse effects on the size or productivity of any marine mammals including sperm whales. Coastal and marine birds are not expected to be significantly affected. Operational activities, underwater obstructions, and discharges are unlikely to cause detrimental effects to Central Gulf commercial fisheries.

There is little likelihood of a well blowout or pipeline break resulting in a major oil spill. If a major oil spill occurs, containment and cleanup capabilities are sufficient to ensure that significant numbers of marine mammals will not be affected. Contact with oil and consumption of oil may seriously impact sea turtles; however, major oil spills are considered to rarely contact sea turtles in the Gulf of Mexico. Consequently, the proposed action is unlikely to have significant long-term effects on the size and productivity of any sea turtle or marine mammal species. Spills occurring in biologically sensitive areas are expected to kill a number of individuals from any or all groups of birds. The net effect will be the alteration of species composition of the affected area(s). Recovery of affected area(s) is expected to take up to several years. Accidental spills could result in a partial, short-term decrease in a commercial population, in an essential habitat, or in local fishing activity.

Socioeconomic Conditions: The MMS expects this sale to add less than 1 percent to Gulf Coast population, labor force, and employment. Employment needs are expected to be met primarily by those currently employed in the oil and gas industry, as well as by unemployed, underemployed, and new employees already living in the area. The MMS does expect some employment will be met through in-migration due to the shadow effect and a labor force lacking requisite skills for the oil and gas and supporting industries. In addition, MMS expects sociocultural impacts to be minimal, with some localized deleterious impacts to family life in a small number of cases resulting from the extended work schedule.

2. Updated Impact Analysis for the Proposed Action

The MMS expects impacts to the following resource categories to remain the same as those estimated in the multisale EIS and summarized above:

- Sensitive Coastal Environments
- Sensitive Offshore Resources
  —Live Bottoms (Pinnacle Trend)
  —Deepwater Benthic Communities
  —Topographic Features
- Water Quality
- Air Quality
- Marine Mammals

- Archaeological Resources
- Alabama, Choctawhatchee, and Perdido Key Beach Mice
- Coastal and Marine Birds
- Gulf Sturgeon
- Commercial Fisheries
- Recreational Resources and Beach Use

Socioeconomic Conditions

The following potential impacts result from the proposed action for those resources where we have new information that was unavailable when MMS wrote the Final EIS for Sales 169, 172, 175, 178, and 182 (the multisale EIS).

Population, Labor, and Employment: The MMS expects this sale to add less than 1 percent to Gulf Coast population, labor force, and employment. It is expected that employment demands will be met primarily with the existing population and available labor force. While an employment impact of less than 1 percent in any impacted subarea is generally low enough to be met by the existing labor force, some labor requiring specialized skills (as is increasingly required for oil and gas deepwater development) is expected to be met through in-migration. In addition, Port Fourchon, identified in the EIS as being a focal stress point for OCS activity, has seen its role in OCS development intensify in the last 5 years, resulting in the lowest unemployment rate in the nation. Even though many industries in the area are offering training programs in the high schools and technical schools to assist in meeting labor needs, Port Fourchon and the surrounding communities are expected to require in-migration, both temporary and permanent, to meet OCS-related labor requirements. Although consolidation of OCS-related support activities facilitated by C-Port 1 and 2 in Port Fourchon and intensified deepwater leasing has caused noteworthy localized stresses to LA 1 and the area's water supply, the range of activity impacts that could result from this proposed lease sale.

Essential Fish Habitat: Effects on EFH from activities associated with proposed Sale 182 could potentially result from coastal and marine environmental degradation, platform emplacement, petroleum spills, subsurface blowouts, pipeline trenching, and offshore discharges of drilling muds and produced waters.

The proposed action is projected to increase canal traffic in navigation channels to and from service bases in Louisiana, Mississippi, and Alabama. This would result in some erosion of wetlands along the channels. Should an offshore spill occur at a platform or from pipelines, estuarine wetlands could be contacted; however, due to weathering and spill response, it is unlikely that wetlands would be contacted. Should such contact occur, it would be light and localized, causing no significant wetland loss. Localized, minor degradation of coastal water quality is expected in waterbodies in the immediate vicinity of coastal bases servicing the proposed lease sale. Maintenance dredging of waterways and channels would result in decreased water clarity and some resuspension of contaminants.

It is expected that coastal environmental degradation from the proposed action would have little effect on EFH. Most EFH can recuperate quickly, but any loss of wetlands as EFH is likely to be permanent. At the expected level of effect, the resultant influence on EFH from the proposed action would be negligible and indistinguishable from natural population variations.

The Topographic Features Stipulation would prevent most of the potential impacts from the proposed action on live-bottom communities/EFH from bottom-disturbing activities (anchoring, structure emplacement and removal, pipeline trenching), operational offshore waste discharges (drilling muds and cuttings, produced waters), blowouts, and offshore spills. Recovery from impacts caused by unregulated operational discharges or an accidental blowout would take place within several years. For any activities associated with the proposed action, USEPA's Region 6 will regulate discharge requirements through their NPDES discharge permit. In the unlikely event of an offshore spill, the biological resources of live bottoms would remain unharmed as the spilled substances could, at the most, reach the seafloor in minute concentrations.

The major sources of discharges associated with the proposed action to marine waters are the temporary drilling muds and cuttings and the long-term, produced-water effluent. Both of these discharges contain various contaminants of concern (e.g., trace metals and petroleum-based organics) that may have environmental consequences on marine water quality and aquatic life. Drilling mud discharges contain chemicals toxic to marine fishes; however, this is only at concentrations four or five orders of magnitude higher than those found more than a few meters from the discharge point. Offshore discharges of drilling muds will dilute to background levels within 1,000 m of the discharge point.

Produced-water discharges contain components and properties detrimental to fish resources. Moderate petroleum and metal contamination of sediments and the water column will occur out to several hundred meters downcurrent from the discharge point. Offshore discharges of produced water will disperse and dilute to background levels within 1,000 m of the discharge point.

It is expected that marine environmental degradation from the proposed action would have little effect on EFH. The impact of marine environmental degradation is expected to cause an undetectable decrease in EFH. Offshore discharges and subsequent changes to marine water quality will be regulated by USEPA NPDES permits. At the expected level of effect, the resultant influence on EFH would be negligible and indistinguishable from natural population variations.

Subsurface blowouts of wells and pipeline trenching have the potential to adversely affect EFH. Loss of well control and resultant blowouts seldom occur on the Gulf OCS (6 blowouts per 1,000 well starts; 23% (of the 6 blowouts) result in some spilled petroleum). In addition, some sediments would be resuspended during the installation of pipelines in water depths less than 60 m. Sandy sediments would be quickly redeposited within 400 m of the trench or blowout site, and finer sediments would be widely dispersed and redeposited over a period of 30 days or longer within a few thousand meters. Impacts from sediment resuspension would be short term and localized. It is expected that subsurface blowouts that may occur as a result of the proposed action would have a negligible effect on EFH. At the expected level of impact, the resultant influence on EFH would be negligible and indistinguishable from natural population variations.

In summary, it is expected that coastal and marine environmental degradation from the proposed action would have little effect on EFH. The impact of coastal and marine environmental degradation is expected to cause an undetectable decrease in EFH. Recovery of EFH can occur from more than 99 percent of the expected coastal and marine environmental degradation.

Due to the protection associated with the Topographic Features Stipulation, offshore live bottoms would not be impacted. Offshore discharges will be regulated by USEPA NPDES permits. At the expected level of impact, the resultant influence on EFH would be negligible and indistinguishable from natural population variations. Activities such as subsurface blowouts, pipeline trenching, and discharge of drilling muds and produced water would cause negligible impacts and would not deleteriously affect EFH. At the expected level of impact, there would be minor effects on EFH.

Critical Habitat Designation for the Wintering Piping Plover: Critical habitat identifies specific areas that are essential to the conservation of piping plover and that may require special management considerations for the primary biological needs of foraging, sheltering, and roosting. These areas are called primary constituent elements and are found in coastal areas that support intertidal beaches and flats and associated dune systems and flats above high tide. Specific areas outside the geographic area occupied by a species at the time it is listed may be designated upon determination that such areas are essential for the conservation of the species.

Piping plovers congregate and feed along tidally exposed banks and shorelines, following the tide out and foraging at the water's edge. They have short stout bills and chase mobile prey rather than probing into the sediment with long slender bills like many birds of the sandpiper family. Piping plovers can physically oil themselves while foraging on oiled shores or secondarily contaminate themselves through ingestion of oiled intertidal sediments and prey. Spills that occur during winter months when piping plovers are most common along the coastal Gulf may pose a threat to the birds. Some piping plover deaths are to be expected if beaches are heavily oiled.

Based on information presented in the multisale EIS, about 18-36 coastal spills of 1 bbl or less would occur as a result of the proposed action. Between 35 and 100 offshore and between 9 and 28 coastal Size 1 (>1 bbl and ≤ 50 bbl) and Size 2 (>50 bbl and ≤ 1,000 bbl) spills are projected to occur. About 4-5 offshore and 10-15 coastal Size 3 oil spills could occur annually in the next 20 years (1998-2018) in the Gulf area. Size 3 oil spills could contact and affect the Central Gulf coastline and inshore habitats with deleterious effects.

Oil spills pose the greatest potential impact to coastal and marine birds. Additional impact-producing factors include air emissions, trash and debris, noise, habitat loss or modification, and spill-response activities. A slick could injure or kill piping plover foraging or roosting along the shoreline. Exposure to oil may cause pneumonia, severe or fatal kidney damage (Frink, 1994), impaired function of the immune system affecting resistance to infectious diseases, and finally, toxic destruction of red blood cells and varying degrees of anemia (Leighton, 1990). Stress and shock enhance the effects of exposure and poisoning.

Low levels of oil could stress birds by interfering with food detection, feeding impulses, predator avoidance, territory definition, homing of migratory species, susceptibility to physiological disorders, disease resistance, growth rates, reproduction, and respiration.

Chapman (1981) noted that oil on the beach from the *Ixtoc* spill caused habitat shifts by birds. Many birds had to feed in less productive feeding habitats. Similar observations were made for wading birds after the *Arthur Kill* spill (Maccarone and Brzorad, 1995). Composition of prey populations changed after the spill. A population enduring oil-spill impacts may have the disadvantage of a long flying distance to habitat of neighboring colonies. Otherwise, neighboring colonies' habitat could provide refuge for a bird population fleeing impacts and be a source of recruitment to a population recovering from impacts (Cairns and Elliot, 1987; Trivelpiece et al., 1986; Samuels and Ladino, 1983/1984). In that case, population recovery following destruction of a large group of wintering piping plovers would likely occur within 1-2 yearly breeding cycles.

The multisale EIS for the CPA describes the potential impacts to birds from oil spills. Plovers and all other vulnerable birds are included implicitly in the discussion. For activities associated with proposed Sale 182, the potential impacts of an oil spill on the piping plover has not changed since the publication of the multisale EIS.

D. ALTERNATIVE B — THE PROPOSED ACTION EXCLUDING THE BLOCKS NEAR BIOLOGICALLY SENSITIVE TOPOGRAPHIC FEATURES

Alternative B differs from Alternative A (the proposed action) by not offering the 70 unleased blocks of the 167 total blocks that are possibly affected by the proposed Topographic Features Stipulation. All the assumptions including the potential mitigating measures and resource estimates remain the same as in the proposed action. The Final EIS for CPA Sales 169,

172, 175, 178, and 182 describes the impacts of a lease sale on these categories. However, the impacts to some resources will differ from the impacts expected if the Secretary adopts the proposed action. These different impacts are described below.

Topographic Features: All of the 23 topographic features of the Central Gulf are located within water depths less than 200 m. These features occupy a very small portion of the entire area. Of the potential impact-producing factors to the topographic features, anchoring, structure emplacement, and structure removal would be eliminated by the adoption of this alternative. Effluent discharge and blowouts would not pose a threat because blocks near enough to the banks for these events to have an impact on the biota of the banks will have been excluded from leasing.

Sea Turtles: The overall level of activity in the full sale area associated with Alternative B is the same as that described in the summary of infrastructure and activity for the proposed action. The sources and severity of impacts for sea turtles under Alternative B are the same as those discussed for the proposed action. However, the major impact-producing factors related to Alternative B that may affect Gulf sea turtles, including structure installation, dredging, operational discharges, and explosive platform removals, would not occur within the excluded area. The effects of these activities would remain in the rest of the CPA and are expected to be primarily nonlethal and to result in few lethal impacts; the probability of an interaction is low.

E. ALTERNATIVE C — THE PROPOSED ACTION EXCLUDING THE UNLEASED BLOCKS WITHIN 15 MILES OF THE BALDWIN COUNTY, ALABAMA, COAST

Alternative C differs from Alternative A (the proposed action) by not offering any unleased blocks within 15 mi of the Baldwin County, Alabama, coast (as of September 2001, twelve blocks were unleased). All of the assumptions (including potential mitigating measures) and estimates are the same as in Alternative A. Impacts for the following resources are expected to be the same as those estimated for the proposed action:

- Sensitive Coastal Environments
- Sensitive Offshore Resources
  —Live Bottoms (Pinnacle Trend)
  —Deepwater Benthic Communities
  —Topographic Features
- Air Quality
- Marine Mammals

- Alabama, Choctawhatchee, and Perdido Key Beach Mice
- Coastal and Marine Birds
- Gulf Sturgeon
- Commercial Fisheries
- Socioeconomic Conditions

If this alternative were chosen, the impacts to some resources on or in the vicinity of the deferred blocks would be different from the impacts of the proposed action. These impacts are described below. However, since only 12 unleased blocks remain within 15 mi offshore Baldwin County, potential impacts due to activities surrounding the deferred blocks would remain generally as described for the proposed action.

Water Quality: Bottom disturbances from platform and pipeline emplacements and removals, rig activities, and blowouts would not occur, and localized, temporary impacts to water quality due to sediment resuspension would be eliminated within the deferral area off the

Baldwin County coast, if the Secretary adopts Alternative C. Additionally, the risk of oil-spill impacts would be slightly reduced in this area because spills due to exploration and development would not occur in the four-block deferral area.

Sea Turtles: The major impact-producing factors that may affect Gulf sea turtles, including structure installation, dredging, operational discharges, and explosive platform removals, would not occur within the four excluded blocks. The effects of these activities would remain in the rest of the CPA and are expected to be primarily nonlethal and to result in few deaths; the probability of an interaction is low.

Archaeological Resources: As a result of the proposal, Federal waters offshore Alabama were assumed to have new exploration, delineation, and development wells drilled. There would be platform installations and pipelines laid in the area. It is likely that some of these activities would occur within lease blocks not considered to have a high probability for historic shipwrecks. The location of any proposed activity within a lease block that has a high probability for historic shipwrecks requires archaeological clearance prior to operations. Therefore, the probability of an OCS activity contacting and damaging a shipwreck is fairly low. However, if an oil and gas structure did contact a historic resource, unique archaeological information contained within a site or resource could be lost. The installation of platforms in the four blocks off Baldwin County, Alabama, would not occur. Therefore, any potential impacts to historic shipwrecks would be eliminated in those particular blocks.

Recreation and Tourism: The major impact-producing factors that could potentially affect recreation and tourism include offshore structures, pipeline emplacements, support services (helicopter and vessel traffic), trash and debris, and oil spills. Exploratory rig activity and platforms associated with OCS development activity could be viewed from coastal communities along the Gulf of Mexico when they are less than 10 mi offshore. As one moves beyond 10 mi from shore, structures appear very small and barely discernable to the naked eye, eventually disappearing from view. Alternative C would defer the four remaining blocks within 15 mi of the shoreline. No structures would be constructed in that particular block. Therefore, any visual impact due to structures in that particular area off Baldwin County, Alabama, would be eliminated.

F. ALTERNATIVE D — THE PROPOSED ACTION EXCLUDING THE BLOCKS IN THE EASTERN GAP

Alternative D differs from Alternative A (the proposed action) by not offering any unleased blocks in an area beyond the U.S. EEZ known as the northern portion of the Eastern Gap. All the assumptions, including the mitigating measures and resource estimates, remain the same as in the proposed action (Alternative A). Twenty-eight whole and partial blocks, all unleased, would not be available during the offering. They are in Lund South, NG 16-7, Blocks 172, 173, 213, 214, 215, 216, 217, 252, 253, 254, 255, 256, 257, 258, 259, 260, 261, 296, 297, 298, 299, 300, 301, 302, 303, 304, 305, and 349. The purpose of this alternative is defer these blocks from leasing until the United States, Cuba, and Mexico (countries that could claim this area) reach an agreement that would define the fate and disposition of these 28 whole and partial blocks.

G. ALTERNATIVE E — NO ACTION

Alternative E is equivalent to cancellation of a sale scheduled for a specific time period on the approved *Outer Continental Shelf Oil and Gas Leasing Program: 1997-2002*. Sales in the Central Gulf are scheduled on an annual basis. By canceling a proposed Central Gulf sale, the opportunity is postponed or foregone for development of the estimated 0.15 to 0.44 BBO and 1.53 to 4.39 tcf of gas.

Canceling a sale would eliminate the effects described for Alternative A (the proposed action). However, other sources of energy would substitute for the lost production. Principal substitutes would be additional imports, conservation, additional domestic production, and switching to other fuels. These alternatives, except conservation, would have significant negative environmental impacts of their own. These substitutes and the effects are discussed in the Final EIS for CPA Sales 169, 172, 175, 178, and 182 and *Energy Alternatives and the Environment* (OCS Report MMS 96-0049, August 1996) and are incorporated by reference.

H. CUMULATIVE ANALYSIS

This cumulative analysis considers the effects of impact-producing factors related to the proposed action plus those related to prior and future OCS sales in the CPA and WPA, State oil and gas activities, other governmental and private projects and activities, recreational activities, and pertinent natural processes that may affect barrier beaches and dunes. Descriptions of these activities and the analysis of the effects are included in the Final EIS for CPA Sales 169, 172, 175, 178, and 182.

Air Quality: Emissions of pollutants into the atmosphere from the activities associated with the cumulative scenario are not projected to have significant effects on onshore air quality because of the prevailing atmospheric conditions, emission rates and heights, and the resulting pollutant concentrations. Onshore impacts on air quality from emissions from cumulative OCS activities are estimated to be within PSD Class II allowable increments. Potential cumulative impacts to the Breton Wilderness Class I Area are unknown. Impacts from the proposed action are well within the PSD Class I allowable increment. However, because of the concern that some of the Class I Area allowable increments may be exceeded, MMS has been working with FWS to initiate a study of the baseline for the Breton Wilderness Area. Questions regarding the types of sources necessary for inclusion in the inventories have been resolved; however, questions remain regarding inventory collection practices and quality control procedures. The intent of the study is to establish a baseline inventory and select an appropriate model to use for modeling the baseline concentration, as well as the current concentration. These two modeled concentrations can then be compared to determine how close the area is to exceeding the allowable increment.

The MMS has instituted a program to evaluate all activities within a 100-km radius of the Breton Wildlife Refuge that could result in potential SO_2 and NO_2 impacts to this Class I Area. The MMS is presently coordinating the review of Development Operations Coordination Documents (DOCD's) submitted by the applicants with FWS's Air Quality Division in Denver. Mitigating measures, including low-sulphur diesel fuels and stricter air emissions monitoring and reporting requirements, are required for sources that are located within 100 km of the Breton Class I Area and that exceed emission levels agreed upon by the administering agencies.

The incremental contribution of the proposed action to the cumulative impacts is neither significant nor expected to alter onshore air quality classifications. The new information acquired since the publication of the Final EIS does not alter the findings of that document nor does it identify any new significant cumulative impacts.

Socioeconomics: Peak annual changes in the population, labor, and employment of two coastal subareas in the Central Gulf represent as much as 12.6 and 9.2 percent of the levels expected in absence of the OCS Program. Although total employment impacts are high, they do not exceed peak levels of activity already experienced in the Central Gulf.

On a regional level, the cumulative impact from prior sales, the proposed action, and future sales on the population, labor, and employment of the counties and parishes of the impact area is considerable (approximately 1.5 to 1.9 million person-years of employment over the life of the proposed action). The incremental contribution of the proposed action to the cumulative impact level is minimal. Peak annual changes in the population, labor, and employment of all coastal subareas in the Central and Western Gulf resulting from the proposed action in the Central Gulf add less than 1 percent to Gulf Coast population, labor force, and employment. However, on a local level, Port Fourchon as a focal point for OCS development (particularly deepwater OCS) is experiencing full employment, housing shortages, and stresses on local infrastructure — roads, schools, hospitals, etc. Any additional employment, particularly new residential employment, and the resultant strain on infrastructure due to the OCS Program are expected to have a fundamental impact to an already strained area.

Essential Fish Habitat: Activities resulting from non-OCS Program events have the potential to cause detrimental effects to commercial fishing, landings, and value of those landings. Additional impact-producing factors of the cumulative scenario that are expected to substantially affect fish resources and EFH include commercial and recreational fishing techniques or practices and hurricanes. Continued fishing of most commercial species at the present levels may result in rapid declines in commercial landings and eventual failure of certain fisheries. These effects will likely result in State and Federal constraints, such as closed seasons, excluded areas, quotas, size and weight limits on catch, and gear restrictions on commercial fishing activity. Space-use conflicts and conflicts over possession of the resources can result from different forms of commercial operations and between commercial and recreational fisheries. These effects will likely result in State and Federal constraints, such as limited access, quotas, and/or gear restrictions on commercial fishing activity. Finally, hurricanes may impact commercial fishing by damaging gear and shore facilities and by dispersing resources over a wide geographic area. The proposed action would add slightly to the overall offshore water quality degradation through the disposal of offshore operational wastes. Other activities of the proposed action potentially contributing to regional impacts would be the effects of potential petroleum spills. The incremental contribution of the proposed action to the cumulative impact is small.

Piping Plover Critical Habitat Impacts: This cumulative analysis considers the effects of impact-producing factors related to the proposed action plus those related to prior and future OCS sales; State oil and gas activity; crude oil imports by tanker; and other commercial, military, and recreational offshore and coastal activities that may occur and adversely affect populations of piping plovers. The extensive oil and gas industry operating in the Gulf area has caused some low-level, chronic, petroleum contamination of coastal waters. If a spill were to occur, lethal effects, resulting primarily from uncontained oil spills and associated spill-response activities in piping plover coastal habitats, could remove a number of piping plover individuals through primary effects from physical oiling and the ingestion of oil and through secondary effects resulting from the ingestion of oiled prey. Recruitment of piping plover through successful reproduction outside the Gulf of Mexico is expected to take up to many years, depending upon existing conditions.

The greatest impact to piping plover is the extent of preferred habitat loss resulting from oil spill and spill-response activities and urban and industrial development within coastal areas. Non-OCS impact-producing factors include habitat degradation; disease; bird watching activities; fisheries interactions; storms, hurricanes, and floods; pollution of coastal waters resulting from municipal, industrial, and agricultural runoff and discharge; and collisions of piping plover with structures such as power line towers. The multisale EIS for the CPA describes the potential impacts of oil spills on birds. Plovers and all other vulnerable birds are included implicitly in the discussion. For activities associated with proposed Sale 182, the potential impacts of an oil spill on the piping plover has not changed since the publication of the multisale EIS.

V. CONSULTATION AND COORDINATION

A. SCOPING FOR THE CENTRAL GULF OF MEXICO PROPOSED LEASE SALE 182, ENVIRONMENTAL ASSESSMENT

External Scoping: On May 21, 2001, the MMS published a *Federal Register* notice and mailed out a special information notice announcing the preparation of an Environmental Assessment (EA) for the Central Gulf of Mexico Proposed Lease Sale 182. In the notices, MMS requested that interested parties submit comments regarding any new information or issues that should be addressed in the EA. The comment period closed on June 20, 2001, and approximately 45 comments were received.

Many of the letters noted the importance of the offshore industry to the State of Louisiana and the Nation. Specifically, Lafourche Parish and Port Fourchon are unusually important to the OCS oil and gas industry. As many as 40 deepwater rigs are being serviced out of Port Fourchon and the activities are skyrocketing.

A summary of the main issues include the fact that (1) increased activity is straining the infrastructure; (2) the area is suffering with a substandard highway that will not be able to handle the truck traffic increase anticipated from OCS activities; (3) severe coastal erosion is eating away the State's hurricane protection endangering the infrastructure and industry; and (4) resulting saltwater intrusion from coastal erosion is impacting the drinking water supply. Almost all the letters indicate that MMS should take a "more aggressive approach to mitigating impacts."

In response to the letters received, Carolita Kallaur, Associate Director of Offshore Minerals Management; Chris Oynes, Regional Director of the Gulf of Mexico OCS Region; Joseph Christopher, Chief of the Region's Environmental Assessment Section; and Stephanie Gambino, Social Sciences Unit Economist, traveled to Lockport and Port Fourchon on Thursday July 26, 2001, to discuss the concerns of OCS onshore impacts. The MMS representatives met with the Mayor of Lockport, Richard Champagne, and his magistrate, Mitch Theriot. The Lafourche Parish Water District No. 1, which services Port Fourchon, is located in Lockport. Mayor Champagne discussed how deepwater demands have increased over the last several years, how increased truck traffic and impacts to LA Highway 1, how deepwater expansion has increased the demand for water and taxed the local freshwater district, and how hurricane evacuation was a major concern due to the condition of LA 1.

The MMS representatives then met with the Executive Director of Port Fourchon, Ted Falgout, several port commissioners, and representatives from BP, Shell, and Edison Chouest. Ted Falgout's presentation explained the positive and negative impacts of OCS development on Port Fourchon. The port provides commercial and recreational facilities, exports some products, and mainly services offshore oil and gas activities. Over 82,500 people per year go through the port, while 200 vessels a day travel in and out of the port. Highway traffic growth has increased from 6 percent to 24 percent according to Ted Falgout. Barge traffic brings an estimated 50 percent of the oil and gas materials and freshwater to the port, which means that bridge openings impact traffic and communities along LA 1. Port Fourchon uses 30 percent of the Lockport water supply, but comprises 1 percent of the serving population. The port believes it is carrying the burden of the nation's energy supplies and that MMS under-estimated the future impacts to Port Fourchon.

The MMS representatives explained (at both meetings) the agency's responsibility to document impacts from OCS activities and that MMS does not have funds to mitigate local impacts. The MMS will stress the impacts to Port Fourchon from OCS development in this and subsequent NEPA documents. The MMS agreed that the cumulative assessment will include local focal points like Port Fourchon in the next multisale EIS. The MMS representatives also discussed the start of a new study with Louisiana's Dept. of Natural Resources. This study will investigate Louisiana's oil and gas infrastructure with respect to a hurricane and will work with Senator Landrieu's office providing whatever information is needed for CARA. For a complete summation of the meetings, please see Appendix A.

Internal Scoping: Internal scoping is an ongoing activity for all environmental projects. However, for this assessment MMS decided to document specifically whether information regarding *resource estimates and oil spill modeling* used in the preparation of the Final EIS for the Central Gulf of Mexico lease sales is still within the range of assumptions used in that document. The Gulf of Mexico Region's Office of Resource Evaluation confirmed that the oil and gas resource projections and associated activities remain within the range of those projected by MMS for a "typical lease sale." The Oil Spill Risk Analysis (OSRA) group indicated that they were improving the wind and ocean current fields into the OSRA model; however, the improvements would yield results no different than obtained in the multisale Final EIS.

B. CONSULTATION AND COORDINATION CALENDAR

The consultation and coordination for implementation of the multisale process began in 1996 and has continued up to the present time. A complete description of all activities and meetings is included in the EIS's for the CPA and WPA lease sales. We have included a brief summary of those events leading up to this EA.

Multisale Process	
May 1, 1996	The MMS Gulf of Mexico OCS Region published a *Federal Register* notice, placed notices in Gulf Coast newspapers, and mailed out notices to governmental agencies and other interested parties requesting comments concerning the proposed multisale leasing process and multisale EIS.
May 22, 1996	The MMS held a public meeting in New Orleans to present the proposed multisale concept. The MMS received written comments from the State of Louisiana, the State of Alabama, the National Ocean Industries Association, POGO Producing Company, Shell Offshore Inc., Texaco Exploration and Production Inc., and The AM Group. Section V of the Final EIS (USDOI, MMS, 1997) summarizes these comments. *All commentors supported the proposed process.*
July 1996	The MMS held public hearings in Houston and New Orleans to receive comments on the Draft EIS for Sales 166 and 168. These hearings also served as a formal scoping opportunity for input on the scope and significant issues related to the OCS Program and to the development of the multisale Draft EIS for proposed Central Gulf of Mexico Sales 169, 172, 175, 178, and 182. No one attended the Houston hearing and only one person, representing industry, presented testimony at the New Orleans hearing. *The single commentor supported the proposed process.*
	The MMS also conducted early coordination with appropriate Federal and State agencies and other concerned parties to discuss and coordinate the proposed multisale prelease and EIS process. Key agencies and organizations included the NOAA, NMFS, FWS, the Department of Defense, U.S. Coast Guard, USEPA, State Governors' offices, and industry groups.

Central Gulf of Mexico Lease Sales 169, 172, 175, 178, and 182 EIS Process	
August 1, 1996	The Call for Information/Notice of Intent (Call/NOI) for the proposed 1998-2002 Central Gulf of Mexico lease sales was published in the *Federal Register*. The required 45-day comment period closed on September 16, 1996. The MMS distributed additional public notices via newspaper notices, mailouts, and the Internet. The MMS received four comments in response to the Call/NOI and one comment in response to the NOI only.

Central Gulf of Mexico Lease Sales 169, 172, 175, 178, and 182 EIS Process	
April 16, 1997	The MMS, by memorandum to FWS and NMFS, requested formal Section 7 consultation for Lease Sales 169, 172, 175, 178, and 182 encompassing blocks in the Central Gulf of Mexico Planning Area. The consultation included all aspects of oil and gas exploration, development, production, and abandonment activities. The FWS concluded that the proposed actions would not jeopardize the continued existence or adversely affect designated critical habitat for federally protected species under FWS jurisdiction. The NMFS concluded that the proposed multiyear lease sales and associated activities may adversely affect but are not likely to jeopardize the continued existence of listed species.
June 23-26, 1997	The MMS held public hearings in Houma and New Orleans, Louisiana, and Mobile, Alabama, to receive comments on the Central Gulf of Mexico Draft EIS for Lease Sales 169, 172, 175, 178, and 182. Few people attended hearings in New Orleans and Mobile. Only two speakers representing industry presented testimony in New Orleans, and one industry representative presented testimony in Mobile. Approximately 60 people attended the hearing in Houma and 19 individuals presented testimony (representing local government agencies, industry groups, private landowners, a newly formed coalition [La. 1 Coalition], and other concerned individuals). *The testimony presented to MMS addressed the following concerns and issues:* *Infrastructure needs of Lafourche Parish south of U.S. Highway 90, due to the existing increased deepwater activities, the proposed action, and future activities.* *Observed increases in traffic (local vehicular traffic as well as heavy truck traffic supporting OCS activities) are placing heavy repair and maintenance stresses on the highway itself and on the economic capabilities of parish and local governments. Additionally, traffic delays are becoming more frequent, as well as increased traffic safety risks due to the volume of traffic and the road conditions.* *In-migration, although it may not be significant on a regional or Gulfwide scale, is having an effect on a local scale and should be recognized as such.* *Freshwater supplies have always been of concern for the Lafourche area. With increased activities, these demands are adding considerable stress to the Parish Water district.*

Central Gulf of Mexico Lease Sales 169, 172, 175, 178, and 182 EIS Process	
November 1997	The MMS completed and filed the Final EIS for Central Gulf of Mexico Lease Sales 169, 172, 175, 178, and 182 with the USEPA. The MMS revised the document using information presented at the hearings and as a result of comments received on the Draft EIS (See Section V of the Final EIS for CPA Lease Sale 169, 172, 175, 178, and 182 for a complete discussion of comments and responses.).
	The Governor of Alabama commented on the Draft EIS, supporting Sale 169, but reiterated his earlier objections, made in comments on Sale 166, to the leasing of blocks south and within 15 mi of the Baldwin County coast. The MMS consulted with the State of Alabama, and the State dropped its objection to the leasing of blocks south and within 15 mi of Baldwin County except for Mobile Area Blocks 826 and 829. The State recommended that MMS delay the offering of these two blocks, removing them from Sale 166 while retaining the option to include them in Sale 169 or future sales after consideration of methods that could provide for the development of the blocks in this area without the installation of new visible structures. The Geological Survey of Alabama agreed to conduct a study of methods that could provide for the development of potential hydrocarbons from blocks in the 15-mi area without the installation of new visible structures on the blocks. As a result, these two blocks were offered with a special stipulation attached, which was developed through consultation between the MMS Gulf of Mexico Regional Office and the Alabama Geological Survey. The stipulation assures that any exploration and development activity on the blocks will be conducted in a manner that minimizes any visual impacts to the Alabama coast (Block 826 was leased.). In addition, the MMS Gulf of Mexico Regional Office agreed to consult with the Alabama State Oil and Gas Board prior to installation of new fixed structures on all blocks in the Central Gulf Planning Area within 15 mi of the Baldwin County coast.
	The Louisiana Department of Natural Resources (DNR) requested the examination of alternatives to areawide leasing based on their belief that such a leasing system would moderate the rate of OCS development. They also requested full mitigation of coastal wetlands impacts caused by OCS-related activities. The MMS responded that it is our belief that current market forces are sufficient to moderate OCS development. The demand for energy is estimated to steadily increase simultaneously with improvements in the technology for finding and extracting oil and gas. Shortages of equipment and labor encountered by the energy industry in the Gulf and the long lead times that are required in developing deepwater prospects will moderate growth as well. Therefore, no

Central Gulf of Mexico Lease Sales 169, 172, 175, 178, and 182 EIS Process	
	alternative to areawide leasing was developed. With regard to potential wetlands impacts, in early October 1996, the Gulf staff met with personnel of the DNR. Although no changes to the mitigating measures examined in the EIS were made, discussions with DNR were productive, covering jurisdiction over mitigation of impacts in the coastal zone, Louisiana's concern that there be no net loss of wetlands, Louisiana's support for and interest in MMS-funded studies, and the potential opportunities for "partnering" in the future.

Central Gulf of Mexico Lease Sale 172 EA Process	
May 7, 1998	The announcement that MMS was beginning preparation of an EA for proposed Outer Continental Shelf Oil and Gas Lease Sale 172 was published in the *Federal Register*. In the notice, MMS requested interested parties to submit comments regarding any new information or issues that should be addressed in the EA. In addition, a special information request was mailed to all affected agencies. *No comments were received from any agency or individual.*

Central Gulf of Mexico Lease Sale 175 EA Process	
April 29, 1999	The announcement that MMS was beginning preparation of an EA for proposed Outer Continental Shelf Oil and Gas Lease Sale 175 was published in the *Federal Register*. In the notice, MMS requested interested parties to submit comments regarding any new information or issues that should be addressed in the EA. In addition, a special information request was mailed to all affected agencies. *No comments were received from any agency or individual.*

Central Gulf of Mexico Lease Sale 178 EA Process	
May 12, 2000	The announcement that MMS was beginning preparation of an EA for proposed Outer Continental Shelf Oil and Gas Lease Sale 178 was published in the *Federal Register*. In the notice, MMS requested interested parties to submit comments regarding any new information or issues that should be addressed in the EA. In addition, a special information request was mailed to all affected agencies. *No comments were received from any agency or individual.*

	Central Gulf of Mexico Lease Sale 182 EA Process
May 21, 2001	The announcement that MMS was beginning preparation of an EA for proposed Outer Continental Shelf Oil and Gas Lease Sale 182 was published in the *Federal Register*. In the notice, MMS requested interested parties to submit comments regarding any new information or issues that should be addressed in the EA. In addition, a special information request was mailed to all affected agencies. *Approximately 45 comments were received from agencies and individuals.*

VI. REFERENCES

Baxter, V.K.   1990.   Common themes of social institution impact and response.   In: Proceedings; Eleventh Annual Information Transfer Meeting. Sponsored by the Minerals Management Service, Gulf of Mexico OCS Region, November 13-15, 1990, New Orleans, LA. OCS Study MMS 91-0040. Pp. 270-273.

Brown, S. 2000. Southwest Economy. Issue 6. Nov/Dec 2000, Federal Reserve Bank of Dallas, p. 2.

Cairns, D.K. and R.D. Elliot. 1987. Oil spill impact assessment for seabirds: the role of refugia and growth centers. Biological Conservation. 40:1-9.

Chapman, B.R.   1981.   Effects of the *Ixtoc I* oil spill on Texas shorebird populations.   In: Proceedings, 1981 Oil Spill Conference. . . March 2-5, 1981, Atlanta, GA. Washington DC: Aperican Petroleum Institute.

COMTEX. 2001. "Oil Prices Up Following Attacks on U.S.," London, September 11, 2001, (Xinhua via COMTEX)

Guo, J., D. Hughes, and W. Keithly. 2000. An analysis of LA Highway 1 in relation to expanding oil and gas activity in the Central Gulf of Mexico. Report prepared for the U.S. Dept. of the Interior, Minerals Management Service, Gulf of Mexico OCS Region, New Orleans, LA.

Frink, L. 1994. Rehabilitation of contaminated wildlife. In: Burger, J., ed. Before and after an oil spill: The Arthur Kill. New Brunswick, NJ: Rutgers University Press. Pp. 82-98.

Leighton, F.A. 1990. The toxicity of petroleum oils to birds: an overview. Oil Symposium, Herndon, VA.

Lore, G.L., J.P. Brooke, D.W. Cooke, R.J. Klazynski, D.L. Olson, and K.M. Ross. 1996. Summary of the 1995 assessment of conventionally recoverable hydrocarbon resources of the Gulf of Mexico and Atlantic outer continental shelf as of January 1, 1995. U.S. Dept. of the Interior, Minerals Management Service, Gulf of Mexico OCS Region, New Orleans, LA. OCS Report MMS 96-0047. 64 pp.

Maccarone, A.D. and J.N. Brzorad. 1995. Effects of an oil spill on the prey populations and foraging behavior of breeding wading birds. Wetlands 15:397-407.

Nicholls, J.L. and G.A. Baldassarre. 1990. Habitat associations of piping plovers wintering in the United States. Wilson Bull. 102(4):581-590.

Offshore Data Services. 2001. Gulf of Mexico Weekly Rig Locator, edition 010907, September 7, 2001.

Rike, J. 1998. Defining social and economic issues for the year 2000 and beyond, miniaturization of petroleum technology. As presented at the Eighteenth Information Transfer Meeting sponsored by the Minerals Management Service, Gulf of Mexico OCS Region, December 8-10, 1998, New Orleans, LA. Information Transfer Meeting Session 1J.

Rose, Robert. 2001. www.oilandgasonline.com. January 17, 2001.

Samuels, W.B. and A. Ladino. 1983/1984. Calculations of seabird population recovery from potential oilspills in the mid-Atlantic region of the United States. Ecological Modelling, 21. Pp. 63-84.

Simmons, M. 2001. www.nolalive, January 2, 2001.

The Courier Houma Today. 2001. Big Share of Coast Funding Targeted Locally, Katina A. Gaudet, NYT Regional Newspapers, July 10, 2001.

The Courier Houma Today. 2001a. Editorial. CARA Bill Can Help Fight Loss of Coastal Areas, June 27, 2001.

The Times-Picayune. 2001. CARA Bill Needs a Boost, Demos Say. July 26, 2001.

The Times-Picayune. 2001. Money Section, August 21, 2001. P. 1.

Trivelpiece, W.Z., R.G. Butler, D.S. Miller, and D.B. Peakall. 1986. Reduced survival of chicks of oil-dosed adult Leach's storm petrels. The Condor. 86:81-82.

U.S. Dept. of the Interior. Minerals Management Service. 1997. Gulf of Mexico OCS oil and gas lease Sales 169, 172, 175, 178, and 182: Central Planning Area — final environmental impact statement. U.S. Dept. of the Interior, Minerals Management Service, Gulf of Mexico OCS Region, New Orleans, LA. OCS EIS/EA MMS 97-0033.

U.S. Dept. of the Interior. Minerals Management Service. 2000. Gulf of Mexico deepwater operations and activities, environmental assessment. U.S. Dept. of the Interior, Minerals Management Service, Gulf of Mexico OCS Region, New Orleans, LA. OCS EIS/EA MMS 2000-001. P. 5.

Woods and Poole Economics, Inc. 1999. The complete economic and demographic data source. Washington, D.C. Compact Disk Data Storage.

WorkBoat. 2001. Vol. 58, no. 9, September 2001, page 16.

APPENDIX A

APPENDIX A

SUMMARY OF LETTERS RECEIVED REGARDING PROPOSED OCS LEASE SALE 182

Many letters note the importance of the offshore industry to the State, and the importance of Louisiana to the industry and, hence, to the Nation. (Note: *italicized* comments occur in most of the letters.)

Louisiana has embraced the OCS industry "with very little fanfare." Its economy is driven by the industry.

Federal Government collects $3 billion plus annually.
Nearly 75 percent of OCS revenues comes from the Louisiana coast.
Almost 20 percent of Nation's energy requirements.

Lafourche Parish and Port Fourchon are unusually important to the OCS oil industry, particularly to deepwater activities.

This gives local infrastructure issues national importance.

As many as 40 deepwater rigs are being serviced out of Port Fourchon.

References MMS's Port Fourchon Study (Keithly, 2001): 60 percent of offshore drilling in next 30 years will be within the port's service area causing a 35 percent increase in traffic on LA 1 by 2007.

Activities at the port are skyrocketing. Past assessments have underestimated activities and impacts.

While lease sale EIS's recognized that Port Fourchon would experience significant impacts due to increases in deepwater activity over the short term, these impacts to LA 1 and the water supply were not accurately assessed (Falgout).

Letters note a general impact and several more specific ones.

(1) Increased activity is straining infrastructure.

Infrastructure includes highways, water supplies, sewage treatment, police, education, and other. Several letters note MMS identified these local stresses in a 1997 multisale EIS (USDOI, MMS, 1997).

Studies have documented that impacts in Lafourche have occurred.

The existing EIS has not properly measured impacts of the 5-year program on the port or parish. The lack of an oil policy further strains this area.

(2) The area is suffering with a substandard highway that will not be able to handle the truck traffic increase anticipated from OCS leases.

The road system is not equipped to handle increased traffic due to offshore oil. Since 1997, automobile-related accidents and deaths brought to Lady of the Sea General Hospital have increased 140 percent.

(3) Severe coastal erosion is eating away the State's hurricane protection, endangering the infrastructure and industry.

Something should be done to avoid serious devastation to the industry from a major storm event.

Much of the erosion is due to oil industry activities over the last 40 years.

(4) Resulting saltwater intrusion from coastal erosion is impacting the drinking water supply.

Despite improvements to the water system, the Water District is concerned it will not be able to fully supply the rapidly increasing OCS-related demands.

These improvements are financed through bonds ($10 million in 1997, $10 million more planned for 2002, and probably $10 million more soon thereafter). The industry does not guarantee these bonds. A hurricane damaging LA 1 could close down the industry locally, leaving the parish population to pay for them.

Early (uninformed) damage to the estuary system is healing as the industry moves offshore. However, this lowers the severance taxes used to pay for local improvements. The healing process can only continue if the demands of OCS activity are met with subsidies to upgrade highways and bridges.

Almost all the letters make the following request.

They write that, beyond the 5-year EIS documentation, MMS should take a "more aggressive approach to mitigating impacts."

Efforts by the Federal Government to mitigate the effects have failed and have been followed by even more lease sales (Falgout).

Assistance is needed to mitigate the identified damages.

The MMS has not addressed or mitigated these impacts. They have underestimated some. What is the point of an EIS that does not lead to mitigation?

The MMS and other Federal agencies should develop a plan to mitigate impacts to landside infrastructure at focal points of OCS activity.

Louisiana shoulders most of the burden of the program while most states refuse to shoulder any of it. Therefore, providing assistance to Louisiana localities that experience these effects is equitable.

A separate assessment of the significance of, and impacts to, the Lafourche Corridor should be made.

Several letters included House Resolution 149 to direct the MMS to develop a plan for impact mitigation relative to OCS lease sales in the GOM that notes Port Fourchon and Lafourche Parish.

Included is a resolution from the Chamber of Commerce of Lafouche and the Bayou Region resolving "that sufficient additional funds should be allocated for addressing the landside impacts of oil and gas activity in the Bayou Region" and that the EA for Sale 182 should address impacts on infrastructure such as LA 1, the water supply, and coastal erosion.

References

Keithly, D.C. 2001. Lafourche Parish and Port Fourchon, Louisiana: Effects of the Outer Continental Shelf petroleum industry on the economy and public services, Part I. Prepared by the Louisiana State University, Coastal Marine Institute. U.S. Dept. of the Interior, Minerals Management Service, Gulf of Mexico OCS Region, New Orleans, LA. OCS Study MMS 2001-019. 23 pp.

U.S. Dept. of the Interior. Minerals Management Service. 1997. Gulf of Mexico OCS oil and gas lease Sales 169, 172, 175, 178, and 182: Central Planning Area — final environmental impact statement. U.S. Dept. of the Interior, Minerals Management Service, Gulf of Mexico OCS Region, New Orleans, LA. OCS EIS/EA MMS 97-0033.

List of Commenters on Proposed OCS Central Lease Sale 182

1. Edison Chouest Offshore L.I.C. — Galliano, LA
2. The Chamber of Lafourche and The Bayou Region, Inc., Larose, LA
3. Lafourche Parish Council, Thibodaux, LA
4. Eugene G. Gouaux, Jr., Lockport, LA
5. Town of Lockport Incorporated, Lockport, LA
6. Reggie P. Dupre, Jr., Senator, State of Louisiana, Houma, LA
7. Laris Insurance Agency, Inc., Lockport, LA
8. J. Wayne Plaisance, Inc., Galliano, LA
9. The Chamber Lafourche, Lafourche, LA
10. M.J. "Mike" Foster, Jr., Governor of Louisiana, Baton Rouge, LA
11. Ted. M. Falgout, Executive Director, Port Fourchon, Galliano, LA
12. Lady of the Sea General Hospital, Cut Off, LA
13. Joel T. Chaisson, II, Senator, State of Louisiana, Destrehan, LA
14. Lafourche Parish Water District No. 1, Lockport, LA
15. A.J. Le Blanc Insurance Agency, Larose, LA
16. Community Bank, Raceland, LA
17. John Breaux, United States Senator, Washington, DC
18. Roy P. Francis, Executive Director, LA 1 Coalition, Thibodaux, LA
19. L. Phillip Gouaux, Lockport, LA
20. Riley Glibs, Board of Directors, Lafourche Chamber of Commerce, Larose, LA
21. Lafourche Parish Water District No. 1, Lockport, LA
22. Heart Center of Lafourche, Thibodaux, LA
23. A.N.S. Engines, Golden Meadow, LA
24. Lafourche Parish Fire District #3, Galliano, LA
25. Elizabeth A. Breaux, Lockport, LA
26. Lafourche Parish Sheriff's Office, Thibodaux, LA
27. Martin Terminal, Golden Meadow, LA
28. Lafourche Parish Council, Thibodaux, LA
29. Larose Regional Park, Larose, LA
30. Edison Chouest Offshore, Houston, TX
31. Coastal Amphibious Services, Inc., Lockport, LA
32. Citizens Association of Bonita Beach, Bonita Springs, FL
33. Board of County Commissioners, Fort Walton Beach, FL
34. Corinne C. Bourg (fax, no address)
35. Lafourche Parish Coastal Zone Management, Thibodaux, LA
36. Charlotte Riche, Raceland, LA
37. Martin Advertising, Inc., Cut Off , LA
38. Warren L. Authemest, Lafourche, LA
39. Barataria-Terrebonne Estuary Foundation, Inc., Thibodaux, LA
40. Loulan Pitre, Jr., State of Louisiana, House of Representatives, Cut Off, LA
41. Domnick LaCombe (fax, no address)
42. Southern Scrap Recycling, Houma, LA
43. Henry J. Lafont, Jr., Larose, LA

APPENDIX B

APPENDIX B

Trip Report
Lockport and Port Fourchon, Louisiana, Meetings on Thursday, July 26, 2001

The MMS received 43 letters from Lafourche Parish, Louisiana, government representatives, businesses, and citizens in response to the *Federal Register* notice's request for comments on the Environmental Assessment for Proposed OCS Lease Sale 182, Central Gulf of Mexico. The respondents stressed their concern for the onshore impacts of the OCS program with respect to the local infrastructure, in particular the effects on LA Hwy 1 and the Lafourche Parish water supply.

In response to the above-mentioned letters, MMS's Associate Director of Offshore Minerals Management, Carolita Kallaur; the Regional Director of the Gulf of Mexico OCS Region, Chris Oynes; the GOMR Section Chief of Environmental Assessment, Joe Christopher; and the GOMR Social Sciences Unit Economist, Stephanie Gambino traveled to Lockport and Port Fourchon, Louisiana, to meet with local government and industry representatives on Thursday, July 26, 2001, to discuss their concerns of OCS onshore impacts. The MMS representatives first met with the Mayor of Lockport, Richard Champagne, and his magistrate, Mitch Theriot. The Lafourche Parish Water District No. 1, which services Port Fourchon, is located in Lockport. Next, the MMS group met with the Executive Director of Port Fourchon, Ted Falgout, several of his port commissioners, and representatives from BP, Shell, and Edison Chouest. The following is a summary of these meetings. The agenda and list of attendees are attached.

Meeting with Richard Champagne, the Mayor of Lockport, Louisiana, and Mitch Theriot, the Magistrate of Lockport, at the Mayor's Office

The MMS representatives explained what the agency does; in particular its Federal responsibilities to document onshore impacts from OCS activities under NEPA through EA's and EIS's. It was further explained that MMS does not have funds to provide local impact assistance; MMS can only provide information and recommendations. CARA "light" was also discussed, and it was explained how the funds are administered by NOAA, not MMS.

Mayor Champagne discussed how deepwater demands have increased dramatically over the last several years impacting the Lafourche Parish community. In discussing the increased traffic and impacts to LA Hwy 1, the mayor explained how Louisiana counts the number of trucks (which deliver supplies to Port Fourchon) equal to the number of cars. Yet, trucks impact the highway much more than cars. The mayor suggested that trucks be counted differently from cars in MMS analysis. The MMS inquired about tolls on the Highway to help defer the cost of repairs. Mr. Theriot explained that a panel had been created this legislative session to discuss giving local governments the authority to place toll roads in their area without requiring State legislative approval. Mr. Theriot further discussed that the LA 1 Coalition had studied placing tolls on LA 1. The results of the study (by Wilbur Smith & Associates) suggested that tolls would only provide 4-6 percent of the $350 million needed to build a new four-lane, high-rise LA 1. In addition, with a toll, there must be an alternative road in and out of the area. This would be the current LA 1, which is in disrepair. Furthermore, while trucks cause a disproportionate amount of the damage to the highway, cars and trucks must be equitably charged a fee under a toll. Port Fourchon, though, is receptive to a toll road and would help to maintain the new highway. Mayor Champagne stressed that hurricane evacuation south of the Intercoastal Canal (the 10th Ward) was a major concern of his and his citizens due to the condition of the highway.

Lastly, Mayor Champagne discussed how deepwater expansion has increased the demand for water. This has taxed the local freshwater district. Despite having made $10 million in improvements over the last several years, the supply is not able to keep up with the increasing demand. Last year Lockport gave authority of the local water district to the parish. Also noted, deepwater (which has plans of five years or longer) does not have a seasonality factor associated with it as does shallow water drilling. Therefore, demand remains constant throughout the year.

Meeting with Ted Falgout, the Executive Director of Port Fourchon, at the Port's Operations Center in Port Fourchon, Louisiana

Also in attendance:
Addie Callais, Executive Assistant to the Port Director
Laney Chouest, Chouest
David deGruyter, BP
Roy Francis, LA 1 Coalition
Henry "Chip" Kennedy, Chouest
Loulan Pitre, State Representative and Port Attorney
Charlotte Randolf, Randolph Publications, PR for the Port
Kenny Robicheaux, L&M Boat/Truck Co.
Peter Velez, Shell
Roger White, Chouest
Greater Lafourche Port Commission Officers:
Irvin "Vin" Bruce, Commissioner
Chuckie Cheramie, Commissioner
Larry Griffin, Treasurer
Jimmy Lafont, Commissioner
Beau Martin, Commissioner

Presentation by Ted Falgout

Mr. Falgout showed a PowerPoint presentation in which he explained the positive and negative impacts of OCS development on Port Fourchon. The following is a summary of the various points made during his presentation.

Port Fourchon is the only Louisiana port on the Gulf of Mexico and the farthest south. The port provides commercial and recreational fishing facilities, exports some products, but mainly services offshore oil and gas activities. Unlike Iberia or Morgan City, Port Fourchon is not a manufacturing port, but an intermodal transfer port. While the port has maintained steady growth over the last 25 years, the rise of deepwater exploration has produced rapid growth at the port in the last 5 years. There are currently 120 businesses at the port, of which a large percentage is oil and gas related. Over 82,500 people per year go through the port to offshore by helicopter, while 200 vessels a day travel in and out of the port (from monthly helicopter logs). LOOP, which is located at the port, provides 13-15 percent of imported foreign crude oil and is connected to 30 percent of U.S. refineries (from LOOP). Since FPSO's will be working in the Gulf of Mexico in the near future, LOOP will become even more important. All of the above facts result in Port Fourchon comprising a 20 percent interest/influence on U.S. oil and gas. The port calculated this number based on the fact that 20 percent of the Nation's oil and 25-27 percent of natural gas is offshore Louisiana. In addition, the port plays some role in 90 percent of the deepwater and 68 percent of the shallow water offshore oil and gas activities resulting in the Port being involved in 75 percent of the total offshore oil and gas volumes.

LA Hwy 1, the only road into and out of the port, divides Barataria and Terrebonne estuaries. The deterioration of the road is extensive due to coastal landloss from wave forces. While Port Fourchon had been active in building up the embankment with channel dredging materials, it is a short-term fix to a long-term problem that grows worse every day. A recent study on the highway, financed by MMS, models a 3 percent low-case growth in daily vehicle traffic along LA 1 and a 6 percent high-case growth. Actual 2000 vehicle growth was 24 percent. Based on a week of traffic count data by the Port, traffic is estimated to increase 13 percent in 2001. According to statistics, the highway is twice as deadly as any similar class of highway in the U.S. (from Roy Francis of LA-1 Coalition). In 1997 the LA 1 Coalition was created to help the parish receive funding for a new four-lane highway from U.S. 90 to Port Fourchon. At present, Golden Meadow to Larose is the only section of the highway that is four lanes. The State and the port are completing an EIS on a high-rise section from Golden Meadow to Port Fourchon, while a corridor study on the section from Larose to U.S. 90 is finished. Michael Baker Jr. Engineering Firm is generating the $1 million study. Funding for the new highway is estimated at $500 million; the State, which controls LA 1, does not have the money.

Barging is the cheapest form of transporting materials to the port. It is estimated that 50 percent of all oil and gas materials brought to the port (mostly liquid bulk such as fuel, water, and liquid muds) is barged down Bayou Lafourche (from the Port's tonnage reports logs). This means that each of the parish's six bridges must open for each barge that goes to the port. On average, each bridge is opened 16 times a day, resulting in impacts to the traffic along LA 1 and the communities: long waits in traffic, missed appointments, increased number of accidents, flaring emotions, and lower quality of life (from bridge tenders' log books). The port has negotiated an agreement with the Coast Guard, who manages the Bayou, to restrict opening the some bridges during the hours of 3:00-4:00 p.m. and 5:00-5:30 p.m. The Leeville bridge, when it breaks down or there is an accident, can impasse traffic for several hours. Considering there are an estimated 6,000 cars that need to be evacuated from Port Fourchon during a storm, the potential for disaster is high (from Port inventory of vehicles).

Part of the increased barge traffic along Bayou Lafourche results from shipping freshwater to Port Fourchon for offshore activities. The Lafourche Parish Water District No. 1, which is located in Lockport, services Port Fourchon. Despite $10 million in improvements from Lockport to Golden Meadow, the water district is currently at maximum capacity. Port Fourchon uses 30 percent of the Lockport plant's water supply, but only comprises 1 percent of the serving population (from the Water District). The differential comes from the offshore demand that the port is servicing. Water consumption for the Lockport Water District increased 20 percent in 2000. The water plant was able to accommodate this increase in demand because Grand Isle no longer needed service from the Lockport plant. In 1999/2000, Grand Isle received its own water line from Jefferson Parish. It is estimated that the water district's consumption will increase by 4 percent in 2001. The water district will not be able to meet this demand despite issuing a second

$10 million bond for improvements for a new larger line from Golden Meadow to Port Fourchon.

Speech by Roger White, Edison Chouest

Mr. White spoke of Port Fourchon's importance to the offshore oil and gas industry. In 1996 Edison Chouest built C-Port 1 ($100 million) at the port. The C-Port's concept is a one-stop shopping center for offshore supplies. It is operational 24 hours a day, 7 days a week. Prior to the C-Port, it took 2-3 days to service a vessel. Today service time is down to a few hours. This results in huge dollar savings for offshore companies. In addition, the companies need to lease fewer service boats because Chouest uses larger, technologically advanced ships. The new ships, which are also built by Chouest, have a 27.5-ft draft. Therefore, only a few ports in the Gulf of Mexico, of which Port Fourchon is one, can accommodate the ships. Morgan City and Iberia cannot compete with Port Fourchon due to lack of channel depth. The port of Venice, on the Mississippi River, has inherent problems with fog and large ship and tanker traffic. Lake Charles has the channel depth but is too far inland. Furthermore, Port Fourchon's primary focus is oil and gas services. This allows the port to concentrate its investments in the area of offshore oil and gas infrastructure. The other ports mentioned have interests besides oil and gas services; therefore, these communities will not continue to invest in oil and gas port infrastructure if the government does not mitigate the negative impacts.

At present, Chouest is building a C-Port facility at Galveston, Texas, in order to service the Western Gulf of Mexico and Pemex of Mexico.

Speech by Laney Chouest, Edison Chouest

Mr. Chouest discussed safety issues at Edison Chouest. He explained how technology is driving deepwater and allowing increased safety. Incident statistics for 2000 and 2001 were distributed.

Tour of Port Fourchon

Attending:
    David deGruyter, BP
    Ted Falgout, Port Fourchon
    Roy Francis, LA 1 Coalition
    Loulan Pitre, State Representative and Port Attorney
    Peter Velez, Shell
    Roger White, Chouest

Mr. Falgout conducted the tour of the port. He began by informing the group that Lafourche Parish has the lowest unemployment rate in the U.S. because of the port and offshore activities (local newspaper May/June 2001). He explained that 90 percent of Port Fourchon's activity is OCS-related, while 85 percent of the 200 vessels that go into and out of the port each day are OCS-related (from port logs of vessels in port). He then discussed some the improvements and changes occurring at the port. Halliburton recently completed a state-of-the-art drilling liquids facility ($15 million) at C-Port 1, while Edison Chouest is adding three more slips to their C-Port

2 facility. ERA (a current tenant), is building a $4 million heliport that will be completed by 2002. Air Logistics (a current tenant) is planning to build a similar facility. Also, LOOP is currently expanding its storage with three large aboveground tanks in Galliano, Louisiana.

Port Fourchon has numerous fuel and water tanks that are used to service the offshore rigs. Mr. Falgout explained that the port must barge water from upper Lafourche and Terrebonne Parishes in order to meet the increasing demand for water offshore. Lastly, Mr. Falgout gave an example of how the port's increased OCS activities have negatively impacted LA 1. The port produces an estimated average of 500-600 tons of garbage a day (from Port vehicle count). The nearest landfill, though, is in New Orleans, Louisiana. This means that 40-50 trucks must transport this garbage up LA 1. Since one loaded 18-wheeler truck is equivalent to 9,800 cars, the impact to the highway is exponential (LA State DOTD).

One-on-One Meeting with Ted Falgout, the Executive Director of Port Fourchon, and Loulan Pitre, the Port's Attorney, to Discuss Impact Issues

Mr. Falgout briefly discussed how the port is managed and how it is financed. The Greater Lafourche Port Commission governs the port. It is made up of locally elected board members. The board appoints the executive director. In order to finance the port, property taxes are collected from companies south of the Intracoastal Canal at Larose to the Gulf of Mexico (the 10th Ward). Forty-two of the top 50 tax-paying companies in the area are port-related in nature. These 50 companies pay 80 percent of the total tax base for the port. Edison Chouest is the top taxpayer followed by LOOP. While the port is making money, it does not have the funds needed (~$500 million) to build the new LA 1.

The Executive Director believes it is carrying the burden for the nation's energy supply but is not receiving any mitigation for the negative impacts. Port Fourchon is a focal stress point and impact assistance is needed. The Executive Director understands that hurricane evacuation is not the way to justify a new LA 1. The way to approach the problem is through an energy security argument. An investment in Port Fourchon for a new highway is an investment in a Federal resource/asset. The Executive Director wants MMS to stress in its documents how important the port is to the nation's energy supply. The Executive Director also wants MMS to reveal the degree LA 1 has deteriorated and how the number of fatalities on LA 1 has increased directly with the growth of OCS and, therefore, the port. Finally, the quality of life in the local community has decreased due to LA 1 traffic — increased bridge lifts, traffic, car fatalities, and highway erosion.

The Executive Director thinks that MMS underestimated the future impacts to Port Fourchon in the last multisale EIS. In addition, the cumulative impact analysis stated that there would be no significant impacts across the GOMR impact area. In the agency's next multisale EIS, the Executive Director wants MMS to be more specific with respect to Port Fourchon's impacts and to point out that there will be significant impacts to focal areas like Port Fourchon in the cumulative analysis. Port Fourchon officials wants to be able to take MMS documents to Congress to validate the impacts/problems at the port as of a result of OCS activity. Lastly, the port officials wants MMS to be more of an advocate for mitigative efforts like CARA and to recognize the need to have mitigation as a part of this Nation's energy policy.

Mr. Falgout pointed out that if a storm came through and destroyed the local infrastructure, in particular LA 1, the price of oil would increase. Port Fourchon affects domestic supply (GOM OCS) and foreign supply (LOOP). If a storm came through the area, more than 3,000 offshore workers, 1,000 port personnel, and 5,000 citizens from Grand Isle and Leeville (south of the bridge) would need to evacuate. In addition, during a storm, offshore companies take valuable equipment such as bagged drilling fluids off the rigs and bring it to safety. This increases the truck traffic along LA 1 during the evacuation process. The port wants MMS to determine how long it would take to get the port and the offshore structures to be operational again.

The MMS representatives explained the agency's responsibility to document onshore impacts from OCS activities under NEPA through EA's and EIS's. It was further explained that MMS does not have funds to mitigate local impacts; MMS can only provide information and recommendations within its documents. With this understood, MMS promised to do what it can for Port Fourchon. It was agreed that MMS will stress the impacts to Port Fourchon from OCS development in the EA for Sale 182. The information attained from the meetings will be included in the analysis, but Port Fourchon must provide MMS with documentation of the facts presented. The MMS representatives emphasized that, while Port Fourchon and its impacts will be discussed in the next multisale EIS, it will not be the focal point of the analysis. Every OCS service and fabrication port must be examined so that a balanced report is produced. It was agreed that the cumulative assessment will include local focal points like Port Fourchon. The MMS representatives also discussed the start of a new study with Louisiana's Department of Natural Resources that will investigate Louisiana's oil and gas infrastructure with respect to a hurricane. Lastly, MMS stated it will work with Senator Landrieu's office providing whatever information is need for CARA.

Mr. Falgout stated that he and the port are willing to work with MMS in anyway it can in order to fulfill these tasks.

The Department of the Interior Mission

As the Nation's principal conservation agency, the Department of the Interior has responsibility for most of our nationally owned public lands and natural resources. This includes fostering sound use of our land and water resources; protecting our fish, wildlife, and biological diversity; preserving the environmental and cultural values of our national parks and historical places; and providing for the enjoyment of life through outdoor recreation. The Department assesses our energy and mineral resources and works to ensure that their development is in the best interests of all our people by encouraging stewardship and citizen participation in their care. The Department also has a major responsibility for American Indian reservation communities and for people who live in island territories under U.S. administration.

The Minerals Management Service Mission

As a bureau of the Department of the Interior, the Minerals Management Service's (MMS) primary responsibilities are to manage the mineral resources located on the Nation's Outer Continental Shelf (OCS), collect revenue from the Federal OCS and onshore Federal and Indian lands, and distribute those revenues.

Moreover, in working to meet its responsibilities, the **Offshore Minerals Management Program** administers the OCS competitive leasing program and oversees the safe and environmentally sound exploration and production of our Nation's offshore natural gas, oil and other mineral resources. The MMS **Minerals Revenue Management** meets its responsibilities by ensuring the efficient, timely and accurate collection and disbursement of revenue from mineral leasing and production due to Indian tribes and allottees, States and the U.S. Treasury.

The MMS strives to fulfill its responsibilities through the general guiding principles of: (1) being responsive to the public's concerns and interests by maintaining a dialogue with all potentially affected parties and (2) carrying out its programs with an emphasis on working to enhance the quality of life for all Americans by lending MMS assistance and expertise to economic development and environmental protection.